UNION

PRAYER MEETING

HYMNS.

"Let the people praise thee, O God; let ALL the people praise thee." Ps. lxvii. 5.

PHILADELPHIA:
THE AMERICAN SUNDAY-SCHOOL UNION,
NO. 1122 CHESTNUT STREET.
1858.

☞ THIS collection of Hymns, prepared by a Committee of the YOUNG MEN'S CHRISTIAN ASSOCIATION, under the advice of several eminent clergymen of different evangelical denominations, is published for them by THE AMERICAN SUNDAY-SCHOOL UNION.

THE want of a small collection of PRAYER MEETING HYMNS has been greatly felt in the meetings which are now being held in various parts of our country, and this little book is offered in the hope that it will meet the want of the Christian community in this respect. It is believed that no collection of hymns in present use among evangelical Christians has been overlooked in making this selection. No one who loves to "serve the Lord with gladness, and come before his presence with singing," will fail to find here those words in which he is accustomed to "Praise God in his sanctuary."

Christian brethren! Sing these hymns with your whole heart and voice. Send up to the throne of the Divine Majesty, the full chorus of praise from glad and grateful hearts. "Worship the Lord in the beauty of holiness," "speaking to yourselves in psalms and hymns and spiritual songs, singing and making melody in your heart to the Lord."

God grant that every voice which shall sing these hymns, may form a part of that glorious choir who shall surround His throne in heaven, and there ascribe "Blessing, and glory, and wisdom, and thanksgiving, and honour, and power, and might unto our God forever and ever."

Prayer Meeting Hymns.

---

1 **C. M.**

"King of kings and Lord of lords."
Rev. xix. 16.

ALL hail the power of Jesus' name!
Let angels prostrate fall;
Bring forth the royal diadem,
And crown him Lord of all.

2 Ye chosen seed of Israel's race,
A remnant weak and small!
Hail him who saves you by his grace,
And crown him Lord of all.

3 Ye Gentile sinners, ne'er forget
The wormwood and the gall;
Go, spread your trophies at his feet,
And crown him Lord of all.

4 May we with heaven's rejoicing throng
Before his presence fall,
Join in the everlasting song,
And crown him Lord of all!

2 7, 6.

"Christ was once offered to bear the sins of many."
HEB. ix. 28.

I lay my sins on Jesus,
The spotless Lamb of God;
He bears them all, and frees us
From the accursed load.
I bring my guilt to Jesus,
To wash my crimson stains
White, in his blood most precious,
Till not a spot remains.

2 I lay my wants on Jesus;
All fulness dwells in him;
He heals all my diseases,
He doth my soul redeem.
I lay my griefs on Jesus,
My burdens and my cares;
He from them all releases,
He all my sorrow shares.

3 I rest my soul on Jesus,
This weary soul of mine;
His right hand me embraces,
I on his breast recline.
I love the name of Jesus,
Immanuel, Christ, the Lord;
Like fragrance on the breezes
His name abroad is poured.

4 I long to be like Jesus,
Meek, loving, lowly, mild;
I long to be like Jesus,
The Father's holy child.
I long to be with Jesus,
Amid the heavenly throng,
To sing with saints his praises,
To learn the angels' song.

3 L. M.

"I know that my Redeemer liveth." JOB xix. 25.

I KNOW that my Redeemer lives:
What comfort this sweet sentence gives!
He lives, he lives, who once was dead,
He lives, my ever living head.

2 He lives to bless me with his love,
He lives to plead for me above,
He lives my hungry soul to feed,
He lives to help in time of need.

3 He lives to silence all my fears,
He lives to wipe away my tears,
He lives to calm my troubled heart,
He lives, all blessings to impart.

4 He lives, all glory to his name!
He lives, my Jesus, still the same;
O the sweet joy this sentence gives,
I know that my Redeemer lives!

4 L. M.

"Whosoever shall deny me before men, him will I also deny before my Father which is in heaven." MATT. x. 33.

JESUS! and can it ever be,
A mortal man ashamed of thee?
Ashamed of thee, whom angels praise,
Whose glories shine through endless days!

2 Ashamed of Jesus! sooner far
Let evening blush to own a star;
He sheds the beams of light divine
O'er this benighted soul of mine.

3 Ashamed of Jesus! that dear friend
On whom my hopes of heaven depend?
No; when I blush, be this my shame,
That I no more revere his name.

4 Ashamed of Jesus! Yes, I may,
When I've no guilt to wash away,—
No tear to wipe, no good to crave,
No fears to hush, no soul to save.

5 Till then—nor is my boasting vain—
Till then I boast a Saviour slain!
And O may this my glory be,
Jesus is not ashamed of me!

5 8, 7.

"Who shall separate us from the love of Christ?"
ROMANS viii. 35.

HAIL! my ever blessed Jesus,
Only thee I wish to sing;
To my soul thy name is precious,
Thou my Prophet, Priest, and King.

2 O what mercy flows from heaven!
O what joy and happiness!
Love I much? I'm much forgiven;
I'm a miracle of grace.

3 Once with Adam's race in ruin,
Unconcerned in sin I lay;
Swift destruction still pursuing,
Till my Saviour passed that way.

4 Witness, all ye hosts of heaven,
My Redeemer's tenderness;
Love I much? I'm much forgiven;
I'm a miracle of grace.

5 Shout, ye bright angelic choir,
Praise the Lamb enthroned above,
Whilst, astonished, I admire
God's free grace and boundless love.

6 That blessed moment I received him
Filled my soul with joy and peace:
Love I much? I'm much forgiven;
I'm a miracle of grace.

6 L. M.

"Whose dominion is an everlasting dominion, and his kingdom is from generation to generation." DAN. iv. 34.

JESUS shall reign where'er the sun
Does his successive journeys run;
His kingdom stretch from shore to shore,
Till suns shall rise and set no more.

2 To him shall endless prayer be made,
And endless praises crown his head;
His name, like sweet perfume, shall rise
With every morning sacrifice.

3 People and realms of every tongue
Dwell on his love with sweetest song;
And infant voices shall proclaim
Their early blessings on his name.

4 Let every creature rise and bring
Peculiar honours to our King;
Angels descend with songs again,
And earth repeat the loud amen.

7 C. M.

"Being justified by his blood, we shall be saved from wrath through him." ROMANS v. 9.

THERE is a fountain, filled with blood,
Drawn from Immanuel's veins,
And sinners plunged beneath that flood
Lose all their guilty stains.

2 The dying thief rejoiced to see
That fountain in his day;
And there may I, as vile as he,
Wash all my sins away.

3 Dear dying Lamb, thy precious blood
Shall never lose its power,
Till all the ransomed church of God
Be saved, to sin no more.

4 E'er since, by faith, I saw the stream
Thy flowing wounds supply,
Redeeming love has been my theme,
And shall be till I die.

5 Then, in a nobler, sweeter song,
I'll sing thy power to save;
When this poor lisping, stammering tongue
Lies silent in the grave.

8 C. M.

"Jesus Christ came into the world to save sinners."
1 TIM. i. 15.

PLUNGED in a gulf of dark despair,
We wretched sinners lay,
Without one cheerful beam of hope,
Or spark of glimmering day.

2 With pitying eyes the Prince of grace
Beheld our helpless grief;
He saw, and O, amazing love!
He ran to our relief.

3 Down from the shining seats above
With joyful haste he fled,
Entered the grave in mortal flesh,
And dwelt among the dead.

4 O, for this love, let rocks and hills
Their lasting silence break,
And all harmonious human tongues
The Saviour's praises speak.

9

8, 7.

"Thou wast slain, and hast redeemed us to God by thy blood." Rev. v. 9.

MY gracious Redeemer I love,
His praises aloud I'll proclaim;
And join with the armies above,
To shout his adorable name:
To gaze on his glories divine,
Shall be my eternal employ—
To see them incessantly shine,
My boundless, ineffable joy.

2 He freely redeemed, with his blood,
My soul from the confines of hell,
To live on the smiles of my God,
And in his sweet presence to dwell;
To shine with the angels in light,
With saints and with seraphs to sing;
To view with eternal delight,
My Jesus, my Saviour, my King.

3 Ye palaces, sceptres, and crowns,
Your pride with disdain I survey;
Your pomps are but shadows and sounds;
And pass in a moment away:

The crown that my Saviour bestows,
  Yon permanent sun shall outshine;
My joy everlastingly flows—
  My God, my Redeemer is mine.

10 C. M.

"We love him because he first loved us."
1 JOHN iv. 19.

THOU, O my Jesus! Thou didst me
  Upon the cross embrace;
For me didst bear the nails and spear,
  And manifold disgrace;

2 And griefs and torments numberless,
  And sweat of agony,
Yes, death itself; and all for one
  That was thine enemy.

3 Then why, O blessed Jesus Christ!
  Should I not love thee well?
Not for the hope of winning heaven,
  Nor of escaping hell;

4 Not with the hope of gaining aught,
  Not seeking a reward;
But as thyself hast loved me,
  O ever loving Lord!

5 E'en so I love thee and will love,
  And in thy praise will sing;
Solely because thou art my God,
  And my eternal King.

11 8, 7.

"A friend that sticketh closer than a brother."
PROV. xviii. 24.

ONE there is above all others,
  Well deserves the name of Friend;
His is love beyond a brother's,
  Costly, free, and knows no end.

2 Which of all our friends, to save us,
  Could or would have shed his blood?
But this Saviour died to have us
  Reconciled, in him, to God.

3 When he lived on earth abased,
  Friend of sinners was his name;
Now, above all glory raised,
  He rejoices in the same.

4 O for grace our hearts to soften!
  Teach us, Lord, at length to love;
We, alas! forget too often
  What a friend we have above.

12 C. M.

"Christ died for our sins." 1 COR. xv. 3.

ALAS! and did my Saviour bleed!
  And did my Sovereign die!
Would he devote that sacred head
  For such a worm as I?

2 Was it for crimes that I have done,
  He groaned upon the tree?
Amazing pity! grace unknown!
  And love beyond degree!

3 Well might the sun in darkness hide
  And shut his glories in;
When Christ, the mighty Maker, died
  For man the creature's sin.

4 Thus might I hide my blushing face,
  While his dear cross appears:
Dissolve my heart in thankfulness,
  And melt my eyes to tears.

5 But drops of grief can ne'er repay
  The debt of love I owe;
Here, Lord, I give myself away,
  'Tis all that I can do.

13 8, 7, 4.

"It is finished." JOHN xix. 30.

HARK! the voice of love and mercy
  Sounds aloud from Calvary;
See, it rends the rocks asunder,
  Shakes the earth, and veils the sky!
    "It is finished!"
  Hear the dying Saviour cry.

2 "It is finished!"—O what pleasure
  Do these precious words afford!
Heavenly blessings without measure
  Flow to us from Christ the Lord;
    "It is finished!"
  Saints, the dying words record.

3 Finished—all the types and shadows
  Of the ceremonial law;
Finished—all that God had promised;

Death and hell no more shall awe:
"It is finished!"
Saints, from hence your comforts draw.

4 Tune your harps anew, ye seraphs,
Join to sing the pleasing theme;
All on earth and all in heaven,
Join to praise Immanuel's name;
Hallelujah!
Glory to the bleeding Lamb.

14 L. M.

"The Lord our righteousness." JER. xxiii. 6.

JESUS, thy blood and righteousness
My beauty are, my glorious dress;
'Midst flaming worlds in these arrayed,
With joy shall I lift up my head.

2 This spotless robe the same appears
When ruined nature sinks in years;
No age can change its glorious hue,
The robe of Christ is ever new.

3 When from the dust of death I rise,
To claim my mansion in the skies,
Even then, this shall be all my plea,
Jesus hath lived, hath died for me.

15 C. M.

"Greater love hath no man than this, that a man lay down his life for his friends." JOHN xv. 13.

TO our Redeemer's glorious Name
Awake the sacred song:
O may his love (immortal flame)
Tune every heart and tongue.

2 His love, what mortal thought can reach,
What mortal tongue display!
Imagination's utmost stretch
In wonder dies away.

3 He left his radiant throne on high,
Left the bright realms of bliss,
And came to earth to bleed and die!
Was ever love like this?

4 Dear Lord, while we adoring pay
Our humble thanks to thee,
May every heart with rapture say,
"The Saviour died for me."

5 O may the sweet, the blissful theme,
Fill every heart and tongue;
Till strangers love thy charming Name,
And join the sacred song.

16 8, 7.

"I have trusted in thy mercy; my heart shall rejoice in thy salvation." Ps. xiii. 5.

SAVIOUR, source of every blessing,
Tune my heart to grateful lays;
Streams of mercy, never ceasing,
Call for ceaseless songs of praise.

2 Teach me some melodious measure,
Sung by raptured saints above;
Fill my soul with sacred pleasure,
While I sing redeeming love.

3 Thou didst seek me when a stranger,
Wandering from the fold of God;
Thou, to save my soul from danger,
Didst redeem me with thy blood.

4 By thy hand restored, defended,
Safe through life thus far I've come;
Safe, O Lord, when life is ended,
Bring me to my heavenly home.

17 C. M.

"I am the way, the truth, and the life: no man cometh unto the Father but by me." JOHN xiv. 6.

THOU art the Way, to thee alone
From sin and death we flee;
And he who would the Father seek,
Must seek him, Lord, by thee.

2 Thou art the Truth, thy word alone
True wisdom can impart;
Thou only canst inform the mind
And purify the heart.

3 Thou art the Life, the rending tomb
Proclaims thy conquering arm,
And those who put their trust in thee
Nor death nor hell shall harm.

4 Thou art the Way, the Truth, the Life:
Grant us that way to know,
That truth to keep, that life to win,
Whose joys eternal flow.

18

"Thanks be to God, which giveth us the victory, through our Lord Jesus Christ." 1 Cor. xv. 57.

JESUS lives, and so shall I;
  Death! thy sting is gone forever!
He, who deigned for me to die,
  Lives, the bands of death to sever.
He shall raise me with the just;
Jesus is my hope and trust.

2 Jesus lives, and by his grace
  Victory o'er my passions giving;
I will cleanse my heart and ways,
  Ever to his glory living.
The weak he raises from the dúst;
Jesus is my hope and trust.

3 Jesus lives, and death is now
  But my entrance into glory.
Courage! then, my soul, for thou
  Hast a crown of life before thee!
Thou shalt find thy hopes were just;
Jesus is the Christian's trust.

19 — 8, 7.

"And cried with a loud voice, saying, Salvation to our God which sitteth upon the throne, and unto the Lamb." Rev. vii. 10.

HARK, ten thousand harps and voices
  Sound the note of praise above;
Jesus reigns, and heaven rejoices:
  Jesus reigns the God of love.
See he sits on yonder throne!
Jesus rules the world alone;
Hallelujah, Amen!

2 Jesus, hail! whose glory brightens
All above and gives it worth;
Lord of love, thy smile enlightens,
Cheers and charms thy saints on earth;
When we think of love like thine,
Lord, we own it love divine.

3 King of glory, reign forever,
Thine an everlasting crown;
Nothing from thy love shall sever
Those whom thou hast made thine own;
Happy objects of thy grace,
Chosen to behold thy face.

4 Saviour, hasten thine appearing,
Bring, O, bring the glorious day,
When the awful summons hearing,
Heaven and earth shall pass away!
Then with golden harps we'll sing,
Glory, glory, to our King.

20

"Great and marvellous are thy works, Lord God Almighty; just and true are thy ways, thou King of Saints." Rev. xv. 3.

HOW wondrous and great
Thy works, God of praise;
How just, King of saints,
And true are thy ways:
O who shall not fear thee,
And honour thy name:
Thou only art holy,
Thou only supreme.

2 To nations long dark
Thy light shall be shown;
Their worship and vows
Shall come to thy throne:
Thy truth and thy judgments
Shall spread all abroad,
Till earth's every people
Confess thee their God.

21 8, 7, 4.

"We are more than conquerors, through him that loved us." ROMANS viii. 37.

HALLELUJAH! victory, victory!
Lift the conqueror's song on high!
Jesus drives the foe before us,
Lo, the powers of darkness fly;
Hallelujah,
Now our joyful hearts reply.

2 Long and fierce has been the conflict;
Long the issue hung in doubt;
Hell united all its forces;
All were foiled and put to rout:
Hallelujah—
Raise to heaven the rapturous shout.

3 Hallelujah—to the Saviour!
Let the triumph widely spread,
'Twas his precious blood stained banner
Struck the raging foe with dread;
Hallelujah—
Satan saw the CROSS, and fled.

22 H. M.

"Blessed be his glorious name forever."
Ps. lxxii. 19.

COME, every pious heart
That loves the Saviour's name,
Your noblest powers exert
To celebrate his fame:
Tell all above and all below,
The debt of love to him you owe.

2 He left his starry crown,
And laid his robes aside;
On wings of love came down,
And wept, and bled, and died.
What he endured, O! who can tell?
To save our souls from death and hell.

3 From the dark grave he rose,
The mansion of the dead;
And thence his mighty foes
In glorious triumph led:
Up through the sky the conqueror rode,
And reigns on high, the Saviour God.

4 Jesus, we ne'er can pay
The debt we owe thy love;
Yet tell us how we may
Our gratitude approve:
Our hearts—our all to thee we give:
The gift, though small, do thou receive.

23 C. M.

"I will joy in the God of my Salvation." HAB. iii. 18.

SALVATION! oh, the joyful sound,
Glad tidings to our ears;
A sovereign balm for every wound,
A cordial for our fears.

2 Salvation! buried once in sin,
At hell's dark door we lay;
But now we rise by grace divine,
And see a heavenly day.

3 Salvation! let the echo fly
The spacious earth around;
While all the armies of the sky
Conspire to raise the sound.

4 Salvation! O thou bleeding Lamb,
To thee the praise belongs:
Salvation shall inspire our hearts,
And dwell upon our tongues.

CHORUS.

GLORY, honour, praise, and power,
Be unto the Lamb forever!
Jesus Christ is our Redeemer!
Hallelujah, praise the Lord!

24 C. M.

"Let every thing that hath breath praise the Lord."
Ps. cl. 6.

O FOR a thousand tongues to sing
My great Redeemer's praise,—
The glories of my God and King,
The triumphs of his grace!

2 My gracious Master and my God,
  Assist me to proclaim,
To spread through all the earth abroad
  The honours of thy name.

3 Jesus! the name that calms our fears,
  That bids our sorrows cease;
'Tis music in the sinner's ears;
  'Tis life, and health, and peace.

4 Look unto him, ye nations; own
  Your God, ye fallen race;
Look, and be saved through faith alone,
  Be justified by grace.

25 L. M.

"Blessing, and honour, and glory, and power, be unto Him that sitteth upon the throne, and unto the Lamb forever." REV. v. 13.

NOW to the Lord a noble song!
  Awake, my soul—awake, my tongue;
Hosanna to the eternal name,
And all his boundless love proclaim.

2 See where it shines in Jesus' face,
The brightest image of his grace;
God, in the person of his Son,
Has all his mightiest works outdone.

3 Grace! 'tis a sweet, a charming theme—
My thoughts rejoice at Jesus' name!
Ye angels, dwell upon the sound:
Ye heavens, reflect it to the ground!

4 Oh, may I reach that happy place
Where he unveils his lovely face!
Where all his beauties you behold,
And sing his name to harps of gold!

26 C. M.

"Worthy is the Lamb that was slain." Rev. v. 12.

COME, let us join our cheerful songs
With angels round the throne;
Ten thousand thousand are their tongues,
But all their joys are one.

2 "Worthy the Lamb that died," they cry,
"To be exalted thus:"
"Worthy the Lamb," our lips reply,
"For he was slain for us."

3 Jesus is worthy to receive
Honour and power divine;
And blessings, more than we can give,
Be, Lord, forever thine.

27 L. M.

"How excellent is thy loving kindness!"
Ps. xxxvi. 7.

AWAKE, my soul, in joyful lays,
And sing thy great Redeemer's praise,
He justly claims a song from thee,—
His loving kindness, O how free!

2 He saw me ruined in the fall,
Yet loved me notwithstanding all,
He saved me from my lost estate,—
His loving kindness, O how great!

3 Though numerous hosts of mighty foes,
Though earth and hell my way oppose,
He safely leads my soul along,—
His loving kindness, O how strong!

4 When trouble, like a gloomy cloud,
Has gathered thick, and thundered loud,
He near my soul has always stood,—
His loving kindness, O how good!

5 Often I feel my sinful heart
Prone from my Saviour to depart;
But though I oft have him forgot,
His loving kindness changes not.

6 Soon shall I pass the gloomy vale,
Soon all my mortal powers must fail;
O! may my last expiring breath
His loving kindness sing in death.

28 — 8, 7, 4.

"On his head were many crowns." REV. xix. 12.

LOOK, ye saints! the sight is glorious;
See the man of sorrows now,
From the fight returned victorious;
Every knee to him shall bow:
Crown him—crown him!—
Crowns become the victor's brow.

2 Crown the Saviour, angels! crown him,
Rich the trophies Jesus brings;
In the seat of power enthrone him,
While the vault of heaven rings:
Crown him—crown him!—
Crown the Saviour King of kings.

3 Sinners in derision crowned him,—
Mocking thus the Saviour's claim:
Saints and angels! crowd around him,
Own his title, praise his name:
Crown him—crown him!—
Spread abroad the victor's fame.

4 Hark! those bursts of acclamation!
Hark! those loud triumphant chords!
Jesus takes the highest station;—
Oh! what joy the sight affords!
Crown him—crown him,—
King of kings, and Lord of lords!

29 — 12, 11.

"Hear thou in heaven, thy dwelling-place."
1 KINGS viii. 30.

O LORD, let our songs find acceptance before thee,
And pierce through the skies to thine uppermost throne;
For thou stoopest to listen when mortals adore thee,
And sendest thy blessings like messengers down.

2 Our Father, our Father, we ask thee to guide us,
And keep us from sin till life's journey be o'er;
Then the last sigh of nature, whate'er else betide us,
Shall waft us to glory, when time is no more.

3 Then, then will we sing the sweet song of the blessed,
And mingle our strains with the myriads above;
Far surpassing all strains that our tongues e'er expressed,
And Jesus, the chorus, and infinite love.

30 S. M.

"They sing the song of Moses, the servant of God, and the song of the Lamb." Rev. xv. 3.

AWAKE, and sing the song
Of Moses and the Lamb;
Wake every heart and every tongue!
To praise the Saviour's name.

2 Sing of his dying love:
Sing of his rising power;
Sing—how he intercedes above
For those whose sins he bore.

3 Ye pilgrims! on the road
To Zion's city, sing!
Rejoice ye in the Lamb of God,—
In Christ, the eternal king.

4 Soon shall we hear him say,—
"Ye blessed children! come;"
Soon will he call us hence away,
And take his wanderers home.

5 There shall each raptured tongue
His endless praise proclaim;
And sweeter voices tune the song
Of Moses and the Lamb.

31 H. M.

"In the day of atonement shall ye make the trumpet sound." LEV. xxv. 9.

BLOW ye the trumpet, blow
The gladly solemn sound;
Let all the nations know,
To earth's remotest bound;
The year of Jubilee is come;
Return, ye ransomed sinners, home.

2 Exalt the Lamb of God,
The sin-atoning Lamb;
Redemption by his blood
Through all the lands proclaim;
The year of Jubilee is come;
Return, ye ransomed sinners, home.

3 Ye who have sold for naught
The heritage above,
Shall have it back unbought,
The gift of Jesus' love;
The year of Jubilee is come;
Return, ye ransomed sinners, home.

4 The gospel trumpet hear,
The news of pardoning grace;
Ye happy souls, draw near,
Behold your Saviour's face:
The year of Jubilee is come;
Return, ye ransomed sinners, home.

32 8 s.

"Having a desire to depart, and to be with Christ."
PHIL. i. 23.

YE angels, who stand round the throne,
And view my Immanuel's face,
In rapturous songs make him known;
Tune, tune your soft harps to his praise:
He formed you the spirits you are,
So happy, so noble, so good;
When others sunk down in despair,
Confirmed by his power, ye stood.

2 Ye saints, who stand nearer than they,
And cast your bright crowns at his feet,
His grace and his glory display,
And all his rich mercy repeat:
He snatched you from hell and the grave—
He ransomed from death and despair,
For you he was mighty to save,
Almighty to bring you safe there.

3 O, when will the period appear,
When I shall unite in your song?
I'm weary of lingering here,
And I to your Saviour belong!

I'm fettered and chained up in clay;
  I struggle and pant to be free;
I long to be soaring away,
  My God and my Saviour to see!

4 I want to put on my attire,
  Washed white in the blood of the Lamb;
I want to be one of your choir,
  And tune my sweet harp to his name;
I want,—O, I want to be there,
  Where sorrow and sin bid adieu,
Your joy and your friendship to share,
  To wonder and worship with you!

33 S. M.

"The Lord will give grace and glory."
Ps. lxxxiv. 11.

COME, we who love the Lord,
  And let our joys be known;
Join in a song with sweet accord,
  And thus surround the throne.

2 Let those refuse to sing,
  Who never knew our God;
But children of the heavenly King
  Should speak their joys abroad.

3 The men of grace have found
  Glory begun below:
Celestial fruits on earthly ground,
  From faith and hope may grow.

4 The hill of Zion yields
  A thousand sacred sweets,
Before we reach the heavenly fields,
  Or walk the golden streets.

5 Then let our songs abound,
  And every tear be dry;
We're marching thro' Immanuel's ground
  To fairer worlds on high.

34 L. M.

"Let the people praise thee, O God: let ALL the people praise thee." Ps. lxvii. 3.

FROM all that dwell below the skies,
  Let the Creator's praise arise;
Let the Redeemer's name be sung
Through every land, by every tongue.

2 Eternal arc thy mercies, Lord,
And truth eternal is thy Word:
Thy praise shall sound from shore to shore,
Till suns shall rise and set no more.

35 C. M.

"Quicken me, O Lord, for thy name's sake." Ps. cxliii. 11.

COME, Holy Spirit, heavenly Dove,
  With all thy quickening powers;
Kindle a flame of sacred love
  In these cold hearts of ours.

2 In vain we tune our formal songs,
   In vain we strive to rise;
Hosannas languish on our tongues,
   And our devotion dies.

3 Dear Lord, and shall we ever live
   At this poor dying rate?
Our love so faint, so cold to thee,
   And thine to us so great!

4 Come, Holy Spirit, heavenly Dove,
   With all thy quickening powers;
Come, shed abroad a Saviour's love,
   And that shall kindle ours.

36 L. M.

"As many as are led by the Spirit of God, they are the sons of God." Rom. viii. 14.

COME, gracious Spirit, heavenly Dove,
   With light and comfort from above,
Be thou our Guardian, thou our Guide,
O'er every thought and step preside.

2 The light of truth to us display,
And make us know and choose thy way;
Plant holy fear in every heart,
That we from God may ne'er depart.

3 Lead us to holiness, the road
That we must take to dwell with God;
Lead us to Christ, the living way,
Nor let us from his precepts stray.

4 Lead us to God, our final rest,
In his enjoyment to be blessed;
Lead us to heaven, the seat of bliss,
Where pleasure in perfection is.

37 7 s.

"The love of God is shed abroad in our hearts by the Holy Ghost, which is given unto us." ROM. v. 5.

HOLY GHOST, with light divine,
Shine upon this heart of mine;
Chase the shades of night away,
Turn my darkness into day.

2 Holy Ghost, with power divine,
Cleanse this guilty heart of mine;
Long hath sin, without control,
Held dominion o'er my soul.

3 Holy Ghost, with joy divine,
Cheer this saddened heart of mine;
Bid my many woes depart,
Heal my wounded, bleeding heart.

4 Holy Spirit, all divine,
Dwell within this heart of mine;
Cast down every idol throne,
Reign supreme,—and reign alone.

38 S. M.

"Pray without ceasing." 1 THESS. v. 17.

JESUS, who knows full well
The heart of every saint,
Invites us all our griefs to tell,
To pray and never faint.

2 He bows his gracious ear—
We never plead in vain;
Then let us wait till he appear,
And pray, and pray again.

3 Jesus, the Lord, will hear
His chosen when they cry;
Yes, though he may awhile forbear,
He'll help them from on high.

4 Then let us earnest cry,
And never faint in prayer;
He sees, he hears, and from on high,
Will make our cause his care.

39 L. M.

"Let us draw near with a true heart." HEB. x. 22.

FROM every stormy wind that blows,
From every swelling tide of woes,
There is a calm, a sure retreat;
'Tis found before the mercy seat.

2 There is a place where Jesus sheds
The oil of gladness on our heads,
A place of all on earth most sweet,
It is the blood-bought mercy seat.

3 There is a scene where spirits blend,
Where friend holds fellowship with friend;
Though sundered far, by faith they meet
Around one common mercy seat.

4 There, there on eagle wings we soar,
And sin and sense molest no more;
And heaven comes down our souls to greet,
And glory crowns the mercy seat.

40 7s.

"In full assurance of faith." HEB. x. 22.

COME, my soul, thy suit prepare,
Jesus loves to answer prayer;
He himself has bid thee pray,
Rise and ask without delay.
Thou art coming to a King,
Large petitions with thee bring,
For his grace and power are such,
None can ever ask too much.

2 With my burden I begin,
Lord, remove this load of sin;
Let thy blood, for sinners spilt,
Set my conscience free from guilt.
Lord, I come to thee for rest,
Take possession of my breast,
There thy blood-bought right maintain,
And without a rival reign.

3 While I am a pilgrim here,
Let thy love my spirit cheer;
As my Guide, my Guard, my Friend,
Lead me to my journey's end.

Show me what I have to do,
Every hour my strength renew;
Let me live a life of faith,
Let me die thy people's death.

41

"Let us labour, therefore, to enter into that rest."
HEB. iv. 11.

HASTE, my dull soul, arise,
Cast off thy care,
Press to thy native skies,
Mighty in prayer.
Jesus has gone before,
Count all thy troubles o'er,
He who thy burden bore,
Jesus is there.

2 Soul, for the marriage-feast
Robe and prepare,
Pureness becomes each guest:
Jesus is there.
Saints, wave your victory palms,
Chant your celestial psalms;
Bride of the Lamb, thy charms
Oh, let us wear!

3 Heaven's bliss is perfect, pure,
Glory is there;
Heaven's bliss is ever sure,
Thou art its heir.
What makes its joy complete?
What makes its hymns so sweet?
There our best Friend we'll meet,
Jesus is there.

42 — 7 s.

"He is able to save to the uttermost." HEB. vii. 25.

DEPTH of mercy, can there be
Mercy still reserved for me?
Can my God his wrath forbear?
Me, the chief of sinners, spare?

2 I have long withstood his grace,
Long provoked him to his face;
Would not hearken to his calls,
Grieved him by a thousand falls.

3 There for me the Saviour stands,
Shows his wounds, and spreads his hands:
God is love! I know, I feel,
Jesus weeps and loves me still.

4 Now incline me to repent!
Let me now my fall lament!
Now my foul revolt deplore,
Weep, believe, and sin no more.

43 — L. M.

"When thou hast shut thy door, pray to thy Father which is in secret." MATT. vi. 6.

FAR from my thoughts, vain world, begone,
Let my religious hours alone:
From flesh and sense I would be free,
And hold communion, Lord, with thee.

2 My heart grows warm with holy fire,
And kindles with a pure desire
To see thy grace, to taste thy love,
And feel thy influence from above.

3 Send comfort down from thy right hand,
To cheer me in this barren land;
And in thy temple let me know
The joys that from thy presence flow.

44 C. M.

"O God, hear the prayer of thy servant."
DAN. ix. 17.

APPROACH, my soul, the mercy seat,
Where Jesus answers prayer;
There humbly fall before his feet,
For none can perish there.

2 Thy promise is my only plea,
With this I venture nigh;
Thou callest burdened souls to thee,
And such, O Lord, am I.

3 Bowed down beneath a load of sin,
By Satan sorely pressed,
By war without, and fear within,
I come to thee for rest.

4 Be thou my shield and hiding-place;
That, sheltered near thy side,
I may my fierce accuser face,
And tell him, "Thou hast died."

5 Oh, wondrous love, to bleed and die,
To bear the cross and shame,
That guilty sinners, such as I,
Might plead thy gracious Name.

45 C. M.

"Hear me speedily, O Lord." Ps. cxliii. 7.

O THOU, whose tender mercy hears
Contrition's humble sigh;
Whose hand, indulgent, wipes the tears
From sorrow's weeping eye;—

2 See, low before thy throne of grace,
A wretched wanderer mourn;
Hast thou not bid me seek thy face?
Hast thou not said,—"Return?"

3 And shall my guilty fears prevail
To drive me from thy feet?
Oh, let not this dear refuge fail,
This only safe retreat!

4 Oh, shine on this benighted heart
With beams of mercy shine!
And let thy healing voice impart
A taste of joys divine.

46 L. M.

"Be merciful unto me according to thy word."
Ps. cxix. 58.

FRIEND of the friendless and the faint!
Where can I lodge my deep complaint?
Where, but with thee, whose open door
Invites the sinner, helpless, poor?

2 Did ever mourner plead with thee,
And thou refuse that mourner's plea?
Does not the word still fixed remain,
That none shall seek thy face in vain?

3 That were a grief I could not bear,
Didst thou not hear and answer prayer:
O thou, prayer hearing, answering God,
Take from my heart this painful load.

47 S. M.

"I can do all things through Christ, which strengtheneth me." PHIL. iv. 13.

JESUS, my strength, my hope,
On thee I cast my care,
With humble confidence look up
And know thou hear'st my prayer:
Give me on thee to wait,
Till I can all things do;
On thee, Almighty to create,
Almighty to renew.

2 I want a sober mind,
A self renouncing will,
That tramples down and casts behind
The baits of pleasing ill:
A soul inured to pain,
To hardship, grief, and loss;
Ready to take up and sustain
The consecrated cross.

3 I want a godly fear,
A quick, discerning eye,
That looks to thee when sin is near,
And sees the tempter fly;
A spirit still prepared,
And armed with jealous care,
Forever standing on its guard,
And watching unto prayer.

4 I want a heart to pray,
To pray and never cease,
Never to murmur at thy stay,
Or wish my sufferings less;
This blessing above all,
Always to pray I want,
Out of the deep on thee to call,
And never, never faint.

5 I want a true regard,
A single, steady aim,
Unmoved by threatening or reward,
To thee and thy great Name;
A jealous, just concern
For thine immortal praise;
A pure desire that all may learn
And glorify thy grace.

6 I rest upon thy word,
The promise is for me;
My succour and salvation, Lord,
Shall surely come from thee;

But let me still abide,
Nor from my hope remove,
Till thou my patient spirit guide
Into thy perfect love.

48 S. M.

"Wilt thou not revive us again?" Ps. lxxxv. 6.

O LORD! thy work revive
In Zion's gloomy hour;
And let our dying graces live
By thy restoring power.

2 O, let thy chosen few
Awake to earnest prayer;
Their solemn vows again renew
And walk in filial fear!

3 Thy Spirit then will speak
Through lips of humble clay,
Till hearts of adamant shall break,
Till rebels shall obey.

4 Now lend thy gracious ear,
Now listen to our cry:
O, come and bring salvation near!—
Our souls on thee rely.

49 8, 7.

"Thou wilt revive me." Ps. cxxxviii. 7.

VISIT, Lord, thy habitation,
Breathe thy peace on all therein;
Peace, the foretaste of salvation;
Peace, the seal of pardoned sin.

Let thy love infusing Spirit
On each heart be shed abroad;
Raise us, by thy boundless merit,
To become the sons of God.

2 Prince of Peace, be ever near us,
Fix in every heart thy home;
With thy sweet communion cheer us,
Quickly let thy kingdom come.
Answer all our expectation;
Give our raptured souls to prove
Strong, abiding consolation,
Heavenly, everlasting love.

50 8, 7.

"O Lord, revive thy work." HAB. iii. 2.

SAVIOUR, visit thy plantation;
Grant us, Lord, a gracious rain:
All will come to desolation,
Unless thou return again.

2 Keep no longer at a distance;—
Shine upon us from on high,
Lest, for want of thine assistance,
Every plant should droop and die.

3 Let our mutual love be fervent,
Make us prevalent in prayers;
Let each one, esteemed thy servant,
Shun the world's enticing snares.

4 Break the tempter's fatal power;
Turn the stony heart to flesh;
And begin, from this good hour,
To revive thy work afresh.

51 11 s.

"Though your sins be as scarlet, they shall be as white as snow; though they be red like crimson, they shall be as wool." ISAIAH i. 18.

O FLY, mourning sinner! saith Jesus, to me,
Thy guilt I will pardon,—thy soul I will free;
From the chains that have bound thee my grace shall release,
And thy stains I will wash and thy sorrows shall cease.

2 Though countless thy sins, and though crimson thy guilt,
Yet for crime such as thine was my blood freely spilt;
Come, sinner, and prove me; come, mourner, and see
The wounds that I bore when I suffered for thee.

3 Thou doubt'st not my power, deny not my will;
Come needy, come helpless, thy soul I will fill;
My mercy is boundless; no sinner shall say
That he sued at my feet, but was driven away.

52 S. M.

"And whosoever will, let him take the water of life freely." Rev. xxii. 17.

THE Spirit in our hearts
Is whispering, Sinner, come!
The bride, the Church of Christ, proclaims
To all his children, Come!

2 Let him that heareth say
To all about him, Come!
Let him that thirsts for righteousness,
To Christ, the Fountain, come!

3 Yes, whosoever will,
O, let him freely come,
And freely drink the stream of life!
'Tis Jesus bids him come.

4 Lo! Jesus, who invites,
Declares, "I quickly come!"
Lord, even so! I wait thy hour:
Jesus, my Saviour, come!

53

"This day is a day of good tidings." 2 Kings vii. 9.

WHERE'ER we meet, you always say,
What's the news?
Pray what's the order of the day?
What the news?
Oh, I have got good news to tell!
My Saviour hath done all things well,
And triumphed over death and hell;
That's the news!

2 The Lamb was slain on Calvary;
That's the news!
To set a world of sinners free;
That's the news!
'Twas there his precious blood was shed,
'Twas there he bowed his sacred head;
But now he's risen from the dead;
That's the news!

3 To heaven above the Conqueror's gone;
That's the news!
He's passed triumphant to his throne;
That's the news!
And on that throne he will remain,
Until, as Judge, he comes again,
Attended by a dazzling train;
That's the news!

4 His work's reviving all around,—
That's the news!
And many have redemption found,—
That's the news!
And since their souls have caught the flame,
They shout Hosanna to his name;
And all around they spread his fame,—
That's the news!

5 The Lord has pardoned all my sin;
That's the news!
I feel the witness now within;
That's the news!

And since he took my sins away,
And taught me how to watch and pray,
I'm happy now from day to day;
That's the news!

6 And Christ the Lord can save you now;
That's the news!
Your sinful heart he can renew;
That's the news!
This moment, if for sins you grieve,
This moment, if you do believe,
A full acquittal you'll receive,—
That's the news!

6 And now, if any one should say,
What's the news?
Oh, tell them you've begun to pray!—
That's the news!
That you have joined the conquering band,
And now with joy, at God's command,
You're marching to the better land,—
That's the news!

54 11 s.

"Grieve not the Holy Spirit of God." EPH. iv. 30.

DELAY not, delay not; O sinner! draw near,
The waters of life are now flowing for thee;
No price is demanded, the Saviour is here,
Redemption is purchased, salvation is free.

2 Delay not, delay not; why longer abuse
The love and compassion of Jesus, thy God?
A fountain is opened,—how canst thou refuse
To wash and be cleansed in his pardoning blood?

3 Delay not, delay not; the Spirit of grace,
Long grieved and resisted, may take its sad flight,
And leave thee in darkness to finish thy race,—
To sink in the gloom of eternity's night.

55 7 s.

"Redeeming the time, because the days are evil."
EPH. v. 16.

SINNER, rouse thee from thy sleep,
Wake, and o'er thy folly weep;
Raise thy spirit dark and dead,
Jesus waits his light to shed.

2 Wake from sleep, arise from death,
See the bright and living path:
Watchful tread that path; be wise,
Leave thy folly, seek the skies.

3 Leave thy folly, cease from crime,
From this hour redeem thy time;

Life secure without delay,
Evil is the mortal day.

4 Be not blind and foolish still;
Called of Jesus, learn his will:
Jesus calls from death and night,
Jesus waits to shed his light.

56 8,7,4.

"He will abundantly pardon." ISAIAH lv. 7.

SINNERS, will ye scorn the message,
Sent in mercy from above?
Every sentence, O, how tender!
Every line is full of love:
Listen to it!
Every line is full of love.

2 Hear the heralds of the Gospel,
News from Zion's King proclaim,
To each rebel sinner,—"Pardon,
"Free forgiveness in his name:"
How important!
Free forgiveness in his name!

3 Tempted souls, they bring you succour;
Fearful hearts, they quell your fears;
And with news of consolation,
Chase away the falling tears:
Tender heralds,
Chase away the falling tears.

57 L. M.

"Behold, I stand at the door and knock."
REV. iii. 20.

BEHOLD a stranger at the door,
He gently knocks, has knocked before,
Hath waited long,—is waiting still;
You treat no other friend so ill.

2 O, lovely attitude! He stands
With melting heart and loaded hands!
Oh, matchless kindness! and he shows
This matchless kindness to his foes!

3 Admit him, ere his anger burn,
His feet departed ne'er return;
Admit him, or the hour's at hand,
You'll at his door rejected stand.

58 L. M.

"Return unto the Lord, and he will have mercy."
ISAIAH lv. 7.

RETURN, O wanderer, return,
And seek an injured Father's face;
Those warm desires that in thee burn,
Were kindled by reclaiming grace.

2 Return, O wanderer, return,
And seek a Father's melting heart;
His pitying eyes thy grief discern,
His hand shall heal thy inward smart.

3 Return, O wanderer, return,
Thy Saviour bids thy spirit live;
Go to his bleeding feet, and learn
How freely Jesus can forgive.

4 Return, O wanderer, return,
And wipe away the falling tear;
'Tis God who says, "No longer mourn,"
'Tis Mercy's voice invites thee near.

59 8, 7, 4.

"My son, give me thine heart." PROV. xxiii. 26.

WELCOME, welcome, dear Redeemer,
Welcome to this heart of mine:
Lord, I make a full surrender,
Every power and thought be thine;
Thine entirely,
Through eternal ages thine.

2 Known to all to be thy mansion,
Earth and hell will disappear;
Or in vain attempt possession,
When they find the Lord is near:
Shout, O Zion!
Shout, ye saints, the Lord is here!

60 L. M.

"Choose you this day whom ye will serve."
JOSH. xxiv. 15.

TO-DAY, if ye will hear his voice,
Now is the time to make your choice.
Say, will you to Mount Zion go?
Say, will you have this Christ, or no?

2 Ye wandering souls, who find no rest,
Say, will you be forever blest?
Will you be saved from sin and hell?
Will you with Christ in glory dwell?

3 Come now, dear youth, for ruin bound,
Obey the gospel's joyful sound:
Come, go with us, and you shall prove
The joy of Christ's redeeming love.

4 Once more we ask you in his name,
For yet his love remains the same,
Say, will you to Mount Zion go?
Say, will you have this Christ or no?

61 C. P. M.

"Lord, save me!" MATT. xiv. 30.

THOU God of glorious majesty,
To thee, against myself, to thee,
A worm of earth, I cry;
A half-awakened child of man;
An heir of endless bliss or pain;
A sinner born to die!

2 Lo! on a narrow neck of land,
'Twixt two unbounded seas I stand,
Secure, insensible!
A point of time, a moment's space,
Removes me to that heavenly place,
Or shuts me up in hell!

3 O God! my inmost soul convert,
And deeply on my thoughtful heart
Eternal things impress;

Give me to feel their solemn weight,
And tremble on the brink of fate,
And wake to righteousness.

4 Before me place, in dread array,
The pomp of that tremendous day,
When thou in clouds shalt come
To judge the nations at thy bar:
And tell me, Lord, shall I be there,
To meet a joyful doom?

5 Be this my one great business here,
With serious industry and fear,
Eternal bliss to ensure;
Thine utmost counsel to fulfil,
To suffer all thy righteous will,
And to the end endure.

6 Then, Saviour, then my soul receive,
Transported from this vale, to live
And reign with thee above:
Where faith is sweetly lost in sight,
And hope, in full supreme delight,
And everlasting love.

62

"Come ye, and let us walk in the light of the Lord."
ISAIAH ii. 5.

WE'RE travelling home to heaven above,
Will you go?
To sing the Saviour's dying love,
Will you go?

Millions have reached that blest abode,
Anointed kings and priests to God,
And millions more are on the road,
Will you go?

2 We're going to see the bleeding Lamb,
Will you go?
In rapturous strains to praise his name,
Will you go?
The crown of life we there shall wear,
The conqueror's palms our hands shall bear,
And all the joys of heaven we'll share,
Will you go?

3 We're going to join the heavenly choir,
Will you go?
To raise our voice and tune the lyre,
Will you go?
There saints and angels gladly sing
Hosanna to their God and King,
And make the heavenly arches ring,
Will you go?

4 Ye weary, heavy-laden, come,
Will you go?
In the blest house there still is room,
Will you go?
The Lord is waiting to receive,
If thou wilt on him now believe,
Thy troubled conscience he'll relieve,
Come, believe.

5 The way to heaven is straight and plain,
Will you go?
Repent, believe, be born again,
Will you go?
The Saviour cries aloud to thee,
"Take up thy cross and follow me,
And thou shalt my salvation see,
Come to me."

63 C. P. M.

"Ye must be born again." JOHN iii. 7.

AWAKED by Sinai's awful sound,
My soul in bonds of guilt I found,
And knew not where to go;
Eternal truth did loud proclaim,
"The sinner must be born again,
Or sink to endless woe."

2 When to the law I trembling fled,
It poured its curses on my head,
I no relief could find;
This fearful truth increased my pain,
"The sinner must be born again,"
And whelm'd my tortured mind.

3 Again did Sinai's thunders roll,
And guilt lay heavy on my soul,
A vast, oppressive load;
Alas, I read, and saw it plain,
"The sinner must be born again,"
Or drink the wrath of God."

4 But while I thus in anguish lay,
The gracious Saviour passed this way,
And felt his pity move;
The sinner, by his justice slain,
Now by his grace is born again,
And sings redeeming love.

64

"To-day if ye will hear his voice, harden not your heart." Ps. xcv. 7, 8.

CHILD of sin and sorrow,
Filled with dismay,
Wait not for to-morrow,
Yield thee to-day.
Heaven bids thee come
While yet there's room.
Child of sin and sorrow,
Hear and obey.

2 Child of sin and sorrow,
Why will ye die?
Come while thou canst borrow
Help from on high.
Grieve not that Love
Which from above,
Child of sin and sorrow,
Would bring thee nigh.

3 Child of sin and sorrow,
Where wilt thou flee
Through that long to-morrow,
Eternity?

Exiled from home,
Where wilt thou roam?
Child of sin and sorrow,
Where wilt thou flee?

4 Child of sin and sorrow,
Lift up thine eye,
Heirship thou canst borrow
In worlds on high!
To that high home,
Through Christ alone,
Child of sin and sorrow,
Swift homeward fly.

65 L. M.

"Cast me not away from thy presence; and take not thy Holy Spirit from me." Ps. li. 11.

STAY, thou insulted Spirit, stay,
Though I have done thee such despite,
Nor cast the sinner quite away,
Nor take thine everlasting flight.

2 Though I have most unfaithful been,
Of all who e'er thy grace received;
Ten thousand times thy goodness seen,
Ten thousand times thy goodness grieved;

3 Yet O, the chief of sinners spare,
In honour of my great High-priest!
Nor in thy righteous anger swear
T' exclude me from thy people's rest.

4 Now, Lord, my weary soul release;
Up-raise me with thy gracious hand;
Guide me into thy perfect peace,
And bring me to the promised land.

66 L. M.

"I acknowledge my transgressions; and my sin is ever before me." Ps. li. 3.

SHOW pity, Lord, O Lord, forgive:
Let a repenting rebel live;
Are not thy mercies large and free?
May not a sinner trust in thee?

2 O, wash my soul from every sin,
And make my guilty conscience clean!
Here on my heart the burden lies,
And past offences pain my eyes.

3 My lips with shame my sins confess,
Against thy law, against thy grace;
Lord, should thy judgment grow severe,
I am condemned, but thou art clear.

4 Yet save a trembling sinner, Lord,
Whose hope, still hovering round thy word,
Would light on some sweet promise there,
Some sure support against despair.

67 L. M.

"All that the Father giveth me shall come to me." JOHN vi. 37.

JUST as thou art,—without one trace
Of love, or joy, or inward grace,
Or meetness for the heavenly place,
O guilty sinner, come!

2 Thy sins I bore on Calvary's tree;
The stripes thy due were laid on me,
That peace and pardon might be free,—
O wretched sinner, come!

3 Come, leave thy burden at the cross;
Count all thy gains but empty dross:
My grace repays all earthly loss,—
O needy sinner, come!

4 Come, hither bring thy boding fears,
Thy aching heart, thy bursting tears;
'Tis mercy's voice salutes thine ears,—
O trembling sinner, come!

5 "The Spirit and the bride say, Come;"
Rejoicing saints re-echo, Come;
Who faints, who thirsts, who will, may come:
Thy Saviour bids thee come.

68 L. M.

"And him that cometh unto me, I will in no wise cast out." JOHN vi. 37.

JUST as I am, without one plea
But that thy blood was shed for me,
And that thou bidd'st me come to thee,
O Lamb of God, I come!

2 Just as I am, and waiting not
To rid my soul of one dark blot,
To thee, whose blood can cleanse each spot,
O Lamb of God, I come!

3 Just as I am, though tossed about
With many a conflict, many a doubt,
With fears within and wars without,
O Lamb of God, I come!

4 Just as I am, poor, wretched, blind,
Sight, riches, healing of the mind,
Yea, all I need, in thee to find,
O Lamb of God, I come!

5 Just as I am,—thou wilt receive,
Wilt welcome, pardon, cleanse, relieve,
Because thy promise I believe,
O Lamb of God, I come!

6 Just as I am,—thy love unknown
Has broken every barrier down;
Now to be thine, yea, thine alone,
O Lamb of God, I come!

69 7 s.

"Thou art the rock of my salvation." Ps. lxxxix. 26.
"And that rock was Christ." 1 Cor. x. 4.

ROCK of ages, cleft for me,
Let me hide myself in thee;
Let the water and the blood,
From thy side, a healing flood,
Be of sin the double cure,
Save from wrath, and make me pure.

2 Should my tears forever flow,
Should my zeal no languor know,
These for sin could not atone;
Thou must save, and thou alone;

In my hand no price I bring;
Simply to thy cross I cling.

3 While I draw this fleeting breath,
When mine eyelids close in death,
When I rise to worlds unknown,
And behold thee on thy throne,—
Rock of ages, cleft for me,
Let me hide myself in thee.

70 C. M.

"The time is short." 1 Cor. vii. 29.

WHEN, rising from the bed of death,
O'erwhelmed with guilt and fear,
I see my Maker, face to face,
O, how shall I appear?

2 If yet, while pardon may be found,
And mercy may be sought,
My heart with inward horror shrinks,
And trembles at the thought;

3 When thou, O Lord, shalt stand disclosed
In majesty severe,
And sit in judgment on my soul,
O, how shall I appear?

4 But thou hast told the troubled mind,
Who does her sins lament,
That faith in Christ's atoning blood
Shall endless woe prevent.

5 Then never shall my soul despair
Her pardon to procure,
Who knows thine only Son has died
To make that pardon sure.

71 C. M.

"Now is the accepted time; now is the day of salvation." 2 COR. vi. 2.

THE time is short! sinners, beware,
Nor trifle time away;
The word of great salvation hear,
While it is called to-day.

2 The time is short! O sinners, now
To Christ, the Lord, submit;
To mercy's golden sceptre bow,
And fall at Jesus' feet.

3 The time is short! ye saints, rejoice,—
The Lord will quickly come;
Soon shall you hear the Bridegroom's voice,
To call you to your home.

4 The time is short! the moment near,
When we shall dwell above,
And be forever happy there,
With Jesus whom we love.

72 7 s.

"The night cometh." JOHN ix. 4.

HASTEN, sinner, to be wise;
Stay not for the morrow's sun:
Wisdom if you still despise,
Harder is it to be won.

2 Hasten, mercy to implore;
Stay not for the morrow's sun;
Lest thy season should be o'er,
Ere this evening's stage be run.

3 Hasten, sinner, to return;
Stay not for the morrow's sun;
Lest thy lamp should cease to burn,
Ere salvation's work is done.

4 Hasten, sinner, to be blest;
Stay not for the morrow's sun;
Lest perdition thee arrest,
Ere the morrow is begun.

73 C. M.

"What shall it profit a man, if he gain the whole world, and lose his own soul?" MARK viii. 36.

RELIGION is the chief concern
Of mortals here below;
May I its great importance learn,
Its sovereign virtue know.

2 Religion should our thoughts engage
Amidst our youthful bloom;
'Twill fit us for declining age,
Or for an early tomb.

3 O, may my heart, by grace renewed,
Be my Redeemer's throne;
And be my stubborn will subdued,
His government to own.

4 Let deep repentance, faith, and love,
Be joined with godly fear;
And all my conversation prove
My heart to be sincere.

74 S. M.

"Lord, I believe, help thou my unbelief."
MARK ix. 24.

LORD, I would come to thee,
A sinner all defiled;
O take the stain of guilt away,
And own me as thy child.

2 I cannot live in sin,
And feel a Saviour's love;
Thy blood can make my spirit clean:
O write my name above!

75 7 s.

"Even so must the Son of man be lifted up, that whosoever believeth in him should not perish, but have eternal life." JOHN iii. 14, 15.

FROM the cross uplifted high,
Where the Saviour deigns to die,
What melodious sounds we hear,
Bursting on the ravished ear:
"Love's redeeming work is done,
Come and welcome, sinner, come.

2 "Sprinkled now with blood the throne,
Why beneath thy burdens groan!
On my pierced body laid,

Justice owns the ransom paid;
Bow the knee and kiss the Son;
Come and welcome, sinner, come.

3 "Spread for thee the festal board,
See with richest dainties stored;
To thy Father's bosom pressed,
Yet again a child confessed,
Never from his house to roam;
Come and welcome, sinner, come.

4 "Soon the days of life shall end;
Lo! I come, your Saviour, Friend,
Safe your spirits to convey
To the realms of endless day,
Up to my eternal home;
Come and welcome, sinner, come."

76 8, 7, 4.

"Come unto me, all ye that labour and are heavy-laden, and I will give you rest." MATT. xi. 28.

COME, ye sinners, poor and needy,
Weak and wounded, sick and sore;
Jesus ready stands to save you,
Full of mercy, love, and power.
He is able,
He is willing: doubt no more.

2 Ho! ye needy, come and welcome,
God's free bounty glorify;
True belief, and true repentance,
Every grace that brings us nigh.
Without money,
Come to Jesus Christ, and buy.

3 Let not conscience make you linger,
Nor of fitness fondly dream!
All the fitness he requireth
Is to feel your need of him.
This he gives you,
'Tis the Spirit's rising beam.

4 Come, ye weary, heavy laden,
Lost and ruined by the fall,
If you tarry till you're better,
You will never come at all.
Not the righteous,
Sinners, Jesus came to call.

5 Lo! the incarnate God, ascended,
Pleads the merit of his blood,
Venture on him, venture wholly,
Let no other trust intrude;
None but Jesus
Can do helpless sinners good.

77 7s.

"Where shall the ungodly and the sinner appear?"
1 Pet. iv. 18.

WHEN thy mortal life is fled,
When the death shades o'er thee spread,
When is finished thy career,
Sinner, where wilt thou appear?

2 When the world has passed away,
When draws near the judgment day,
When the awful trump shall sound,
Say, oh, where wilt thou be found?

3 What shall soothe thy bursting heart,
When the saints and thou must part?
When the good with joy are crowned,
Sinner, where wilt thou be found?

4 While the Holy Ghost is nigh,
Quickly to the Saviour fly;
Then shall peace thy spirit cheer,
Then in heaven shalt thou appear.

78 L. M.

"We rejoice in the hope of the glory of God."
ROMANS V. 2.

STAND up, my soul, shake off thy fears,
And gird the Gospel armour on;
March to the gates of endless joy,
Where Jesus, thy great Captain's gone.

2 Hell and thy sins resist thy course;
But hell and sin are vanquished foes;
Thy Saviour nailed them to the cross,
And sung the triumph when he rose.

3 Then let my soul march boldly on,
Press forward to the heavenly gate;
There peace and joy eternal reign,
And glittering robes for conquerors wait.

4 There shall I wear a starry crown,
And triumph in Almighty grace,
While all the armies of the skies
Join in my glorious Leader's praise.

79 C. M.

"The gift of God is eternal life through Jesus Christ our Lord." ROMANS vi. 23.

WHEN I can read my title clear
To mansions in the skies,
I'll bid farewell to every fear
And wipe my weeping eyes.

2 Should earth against my soul engage
And fiery darts be hurled,
Then I can smile at Satan's rage
And face a frowning world.

3 Let cares like a wild deluge come,
And storms of sorrow fall;
May I but safely reach my home,
My God, my heaven, my all.

4 There shall I bathe my weary soul
In seas of heavenly rest,
And not a wave of trouble roll
Across my peaceful breast.

80 7 s.

"Rejoice in the Lord alway." PHIL. iv. 4.

CHILDREN of the heavenly King!
As ye journey, sweetly sing;
Sing your Saviour's worthy praise,
Glorious in his works and ways.

2 Ye are travelling home to God,
In the way the fathers trod;
They are happy now, and ye
Soon their happiness shall see.

3 Shout, ye little flock, and blest;
You on Jesus' throne shall rest;
There, your seat is now prepared,—
There, your kingdom and reward.

4 Fear not, brethren, joyful stand
On the borders of your land;
Jesus Christ, your Father's Son,
Bids you undismayed go on.

5 Lord, submissive make us go,
Gladly leaving all below;
Only thou our leader be,
And we still will follow thee.

81 S. M.

"By grace ye are saved through faith." EPH. ii. 8.

GRACE! 'tis a charming sound,
Harmonious to the ear;
Heaven with the echo shall resound,
And all the earth shall hear.

2 Grace first contrived a way
To save rebellious man,
And all the means that grace display,
Which drew the wondrous plan.

3 Grace guides my wandering feet
To tread the heavenly road;
And new supplies each hour I meet
While pressing on to God.

4 Grace all the work shall crown
Through everlasting days;
It lays in heaven the topmost stone,
And well deserves the praise.

82 L. M.

"Consider the Apostle and High-Priest of our profession, Christ Jesus." HEB. iii. 1.

WHEN gathering clouds around I view,
And days are dark and friends are few,
On him I lean, who, not in vain,
Experienced every human pain;
He sees my wants, allays my fears,
And counts and treasures up my tears.

2 If aught should tempt my soul to stray
From heavenly virtue's narrow way,
To fly the good I should pursue,
Or do the sin I should not do;
Still he, who felt temptation's power,
Shall guard me in that dangerous hour.

3 And O, when I have safely past
Through every conflict but the last,
Still, still unchanging, watch beside
My bed of death, for thou hast died;
Then point to realms of cloudless day,
And wipe the latest tear away.

83 C. M.

"The entrance of thy words giveth light; it giveth understanding unto the simple." Ps. cxix. 130.

ALMIGHTY GOD! thy word is cast
Like seed into the ground;
Now let the dew of heaven descend,
And righteous fruits abound.

2 Let not the foe of Christ and man
This holy seed remove;
But give it root in every heart,
To bring forth fruits of love.

3 Let not the world's deceitful cares
The rising plant destroy;
But let it yield a hundred fold,
The fruits of peace and joy.

4 Oft as the precious seed is sown,
Thy quickening grace bestow,
That all whose souls the truth receive,
Its saving power may know.

84 C. M.

"Thy word is a lamp unto my feet, and a light unto my path." Ps. cxix. 105.

FATHER of mercies, in thy word,
What endless glory shines!
Forever be thy name adored
For these celestial lines.

2 Here the Redeemer's welcome voice
Spreads heavenly peace around,
And life, and everlasting joys
Attend the blissful sound.

3 O, may these heavenly pages be
My ever dear delight;
And still new beauties may I see,
And still increasing light!

4 Divine Instructor, gracious Lord,
Be thou forever near,
Teach me to love thy sacred word,
And view my Saviour there.

85 S. M.

"My times are in thy hand." Ps. xxxi. 15.

MY times are in thy hand;
My God, I wish them there;
My life, my friends, my soul I leave
Entirely to thy care.

2 My times are in thy hand,
Whatever they may be;
Pleasing or painful, dark or bright,
As best may seem to thee.

3 My times are in thy hand:
Why should I doubt or fear?
My Father's hand will never cause
His child a needless tear.

4 My times are in thy hand,
Jesus, my Advocate;
Nor shall thy hand be stretched in vain,
For me to supplicate.

5 My times are in thy hand;
I'll always trust in thee;
And after death, at thy right hand
I shall forever be.

86 C. M.

"Not what I will, but what thou wilt." MARK xiv. 36.

FATHER, whate'er of earthly bliss
Thy sovereign will denies,
Accepted at thy throne of grace,
Let this petition rise:—

2 "Give me a calm, a thankful heart,
From every murmur free;
The blessings of thy grace impart,
And make me live to thee.

3 "Let the sweet hope that I am thine,
My life and death attend;
Thy presence through my journey shine,
And crown my journey's end."

87 L. M.

"The Lord is the portion of my inheritance." Ps. xvi. 5.

WHAT sinners value I resign;
Lord, 'tis enough that thou art mine;
I shall behold thy blissful face,
And stand complete in righteousness.

2 This life's a dream, an empty show;
But the bright world to which I go
Hath joys substantial and sincere;
When shall I wake and find me there?

3 O glorious hour! O blest abode!
I shall be near and like my God!
And flesh and sin no more control
The sacred pleasures of the soul.

88 C. M.

"I will run the way of thy commandments."
Ps. cxix. 32.

IN all my Lord's appointed ways,
My journey I'll pursue;
Hinder me not, ye much loved saints,
For I must go with you.

2 Through floods and flames, if Jesus leads
I'll follow where he goes;
Hinder me not, shall be my cry,
Though earth and hell oppose.

3 Through duty and through trials too,
I'll go at his command:
Hinder me not, for I am bound
To my Immanuel's land.

4 And when my Saviour calls me home,
Still this my cry shall be,
Hinder me not, come, welcome, death,
I'll gladly go with thee.

89 C. M.

"Being justified freely by his grace." ROMANS iii. 24.

AMAZING grace! how sweet the sound
That saved a wretch like me!
I once was lost, but now am found,
Was blind, but now I see.

2 'Twas grace that taught my heart to fear,
And grace my fears relieved:
How precious did that grace appear,
The hour I first believed.

3 Through many dangers, toils, and snares
I have already come:
'Tis grace that brought me safe thus far,
And grace will lead me home.

4 And when this flesh and heart shall fail,
And mortal life shall cease,
I shall possess, within the vail,
A life of joy and peace.

90 L. M.

"So run that ye may obtain." 1 Cor. ix. 24.

AWAKE, our souls; away our fears;
Let every trembling thought be gone;
Awake, and run the heavenly race,
And put a cheerful courage on.

2 True, 'tis a strait and thorny road,
And mortal spirits tire and faint;
But they forget the mighty God,
Who feeds the strength of every saint

3 From thee, the overflowing Spring,
Our souls shall drink a full supply;
While those who trust their native strength
Shall melt away, and droop, and die.

4 Swift as an eagle cuts the air,
We'll mount aloft to thine abode;
On wings of love our souls shall fly,
Nor tire amid the heavenly road.

91 C. M.

"I press towards the mark for the prize of the high calling of God in Christ Jesus." PHIL. iii. 14.

AWAKE, my soul, stretch every nerve,
And press with vigour on:
A heavenly race demands thy zeal,
And an immortal crown.

2 A cloud of witnesses around
Hold thee in full survey;
Forget the steps already trod,
And onward urge thy way.

3 'Tis God's all animating voice,
That calls thee from on high,
'Tis his own hand presents the prize
To thine uplifted eye.

4 Then wake, my soul, stretch every nerve,
And press with vigour on;
A heavenly race demands thy zeal,
And an immortal crown.

92 S. M.

"By the grace of our Lord Jesus Christ we shall be saved." ACTS xv. 11.

A SINNER saved by grace!
No other hope is mine,
Than thus to see my Father's face,
And in his glory shine.

2 No merits of my own,
No righteousness I bring,
With broken, contrite heart, alone
To Jesus' cross I cling.

3 I know he will forgive
My sins, if thus I come;
I know that I at last shall live
With him in heaven, my home.

93 C. M.

"Return unto the Lord, and he will have mercy; and to our God, for he will abundantly pardon." ISAIAH lv. 7.

HOW oft, alas! this wretched heart
Has wandered from the Lord:
How oft my roving thoughts depart,
Forgetful of his word.

2 Yet sovereign mercy calls, "Return;"
Dear Lord, and may I come?
My vile ingratitude I mourn;
O, take the wanderer home.

3 And canst thou, wilt thou yet forgive
And bid my crimes remove?
And shall a pardoned rebel live
To speak thy wondrous love?

4 Almighty grace, thy healing power,
How glorious, how divine;
That can to life and bliss restore
So vile a heart as mine.

5 Thy pardoning love, so free, so sweet,
Dear Saviour, I adore:
O keep me at thy sacred feet,
And let me rove no more.

94 8, 7, 4.

"Why art thou cast down, O my soul?" Ps. xlii. 5.

O MY soul, what means this sadness?
Wherefore art thou thus cast down?
Let thy grief be turned to gladness;
Bid thy restless fears begone;
Look to Jesus,
And rejoice in his dear name.

2 Though ten thousand ills beset thee,
From without and from within,
Jesus says he'll ne'er forget thee,
But will save from hell and sin:
He is faithful
To perform his gracious word.

3 Though distresses now attend thee,
And thou tread'st the thorny road,
His right hand shall still defend thee,
Soon he'll bring thee home to God!
Thou shalt praise him,
Praise the great Redeemer's name.

95 S. M.

"Trust ye in the Lord forever." ISAIAH xxvi. 4.

GIVE to the winds thy fears,
Hope, and be undismayed;
God hears thy sighs and counts thy tears,
God shall lift up thy head.

2 Through waves, and clouds, and storms,
He gently clears the way;
Wait thou his time; so shall this night
Soon end in joyous day.

3 Still heavy is thy heart?
Still sink thy spirits down?
Cast off the weight, let fear depart,
And every care begone.

4 What though thou rulest not?
Yet heaven, and earth, and hell
Proclaim God sitteth on the throne,
And ruleth all things well.

5 Leave to his sovereign sway,
To choose and to command;
So shalt thou, wondering, own his way
How wise, how good his hand!

96

"I have put my trust in the Lord God." Ps. lxxiii. 28.

BEGONE, unbelief!
My Saviour is near;
And for my relief
Will surely appear:
By prayer let me wrestle,
And he will perform;
With Christ in the vessel,
I smile at the storm.

2 Determined to save,
He watched o'er my path,
When Satan's blind slave
I sported with death:

And can he have taught me
  To trust in his name,
And thus far have brought me
  To put me to shame?

3 Why should I complain
  Of want or distress,
Temptation or pain?
  He told me no less:
The heirs of salvation,
  I know from his word,
Through much tribulation
  Must follow their Lord.

4 Though dark be my way,
  Since he is my guide,
'Tis mine to obey,
  'Tis his to provide:
His way was much rougher
  And darker than mine;
Did Jesus thus suffer,
  And shall I repine?

5 His love in time past
  Forbids me to think
He'll leave me at last
  In trouble to sink:
Though painful at present,
  'Twill cease before long,
And then, O how pleasant
  The conqueror's song!

97 L. M.

"Now faith is the substance of things hoped for, the evidence of things not seen." HEB. xi. 1.

AS when the weary traveller gains
The height of some o'erlooking hill,
His heart revives, if, o'er the plains,
He sees his home though distant still:

2 So when the Christian pilgrim views
By faith his mansion in the skies;
The sight his fainting strength renews,
And wings his speed to reach the prize.

3 'Tis there, he says, I am to dwell
With Jesus in the realms of day:
Then I shall bid my cares farewell,
And he will wipe my tears away.

98 7, 6.

"Jesus Christ and him crucified." 1 COR. ii. 2.

VAIN, delusive world, adieu,
With all of creature good;
Only Jesus I pursue,
Who bought me with his blood;
All thy pleasures I forego,
All thy wealth, and all thy pride,
Only Jesus will I know,
And Jesus crucified.

2 Him to know is life and peace,
And pleasure without end,
This is all my happiness,
On Jesus to depend:

Daily in his grace to grow,
And ever in his love abide;
Only Jesus will I know,
And Jesus crucified.

3 O that I could all invite,
This saving truth to prove;
Show the length, the breadth, the height,
And depth of Jesus' love;
Fain I would to sinners show
His blood by faith alone applied,
Only Jesus will I know,
And Jesus crucified.

99 C. P. M.

"The darkness is past, and the true light now shineth."
1 JOHN ii. 8.

TELL me no more of earthly toys,
Of sinful mirth and carnal joys,
The things I loved before;
Let me but view my Saviour's face,
And feel his animating grace,
And I desire no more.

2 Tell me no more of fame and wealth,
Of careless ease and blooming health,
For they have all their snares;
Let me but know my sins forgiven,
And see my name enrolled in heaven,
And I am free from cares.

100 S. M.

"Watch." MATT. xxv. 13.

A CHARGE to keep I have,
  A God to glorify;
A never dying soul to save,
  And fit it for the sky.

2 To serve the present age,
  My calling to fulfil,
O, may it all my powers engage
  To do my Master's will.

3 Arm me with jealous care,
  As in thy sight to live;
And O, thy servant, Lord, prepare
  A strict account to give.

4 Help me to watch and pray,
  And on thyself rely,
Assured, if I my trust betray,
  I shall forever die.

101 C. M.

"Fight the good fight of faith." 1 TIM. vi. 12.

AM I a soldier of the cross,
  A follower of the Lamb?
And shall I fear to own his cause,
  Or blush to speak his name?

2 Shall I be carried to the skies
  On flowery beds of ease?
While others fought to win the prize,
  And sailed through bloody seas.

3 Are there no foes for me to face,
Must I not stem the flood?
Is this vain world a friend to grace,
To help me on to God?

4 Sure I must fight if I would reign,
Increase my courage, Lord!
I'll bear the toil, endure the pain,
Supported by thy word.

5 Thy saints in all this glorious war
Shall conquer though they die;
They see the triumph from afar,
By faith they bring it nigh.

6 When that illustrious day shall rise,
And all thy armies shine
In robes of victory through the skies,
The glory shall be thine.

102 — 7s.

"In the shadow of thy wings will I make my refuge."
Ps. lvii. 1.

JESUS, lover of my soul!
Let me to thy bosom fly,
While the billows near me roll,
While the tempest still is high;
Hide me, O my Saviour, hide
Till the storm of life be past!
Safe into the haven guide;
O! receive my soul at last.

2 Other refuge have I none,—
Hangs my helpless soul on thee:
Leave, ah! leave me not alone;
Still support and comfort me:
All my trust on thee is stayed;
All my help from thee I bring:
Cover my defenceless head
With the shadow of thy wing.

3 Plenteous grace with thee is found,
Grace to pardon all my sin;
Let the healing streams abound,
Make and keep me pure within;
Thou of life the fountain art,
Freely let me take of thee;
Spring thou up within my heart,
Rise to all eternity.

103 11 s.

"The rock of my strength, and my refuge, is in God."
Ps. lxii. 7.

HOW firm a foundation, ye saints of the Lord,
Is laid for your faith in his excellent word;
What more can he say than to you he hath said,
You who unto Jesus for refuge have fled:

2 Fear not, I am with thee, O be not dismayed,
I, I am thy God, and will still give thee aid;

I'll strengthen thee, help thee, and cause
thee to stand,
Upheld by my righteous, omnipotent hand.

3 When through the deep waters I call thee
to go,
The rivers of woe shall not thee over-
flow;
For I will be with thee, thy troubles to
bless,
And sanctify to thee thy deepest distress.

4 When through fiery trials thy pathway
shall lie,
My grace, all sufficient, shall be thy
supply;
The flame shall not hurt thee, I only design
Thy dross to consume, and thy gold to
refine.

5 The soul that to Jesus has fled for repose,
I will not, I will not desert to his foes;
That soul, though all hell shall endeavour
to shake,
I'll never,—no, never,—no, never forsake.

104 C. M.

"By the grace of God, I am what I am."
1 Cor. xv. 10.

ALL that I was, my sin, my guilt,
My death, was all my own;
All that I am, I owe to thee,
My gracious God alone.

2 The evil of my former state
  Was mine, and only mine;
The good in which I now rejoice
  Is thine, and only thine.

3 The darkness of my former state,
  The bondage, all was mine;
The light of life in which I walk,
  The liberty, is thine.

4 Thy grace first made me feel my sin,
  And taught me to believe;
Then in believing, peace I found,
  And now I live, I live.

5 All that I am, e'en here on earth,
  All that I hope to be
When Jesus comes, and glory dawns,
  I owe it, Lord, to thee.

105 C. M.

"We loved him, because he first loved us."
1 JOHN iv. 19.

WE love thee, Lord, because when we
  Had erred and gone astray,
Thou didst recall our wandering souls
  Into the homeward way.
When helpless, hopeless, we were lost
  In sin and sorrow's night,
Thou didst send forth a guiding ray
  Of thy benignant light.

2 Because when we forsook thy ways,
Nor kept thy holy will,
Thou wert not an avenging Judge,
But a gracious Father still.
Because we have forgot thee, Lord,
But thou hast not forgot,—
Because we have forsaken thee,
But thou forsakest not;

3 Because, O Lord, thou lovedst us
With everlasting love;
Because thou gav'st thy Son to die,
That we might live above;
Because when we were heirs of wrath,
Thou gav'st the hopes of heaven;
We love because we much have sinned,
And much have been forgiven.

106

"Now is our salvation nearer than when we believed."
ROMANS xiii. 11.

COME, let us anew
Our journey pursue,
Roll round with the year,
And never stand still till the Master appear.
His adorable will
Let us gladly fulfil,
And our talents improve
By the patience of hope and the labour of love.

2 Our life is a dream;
Our time, as a stream,
Glides swiftly away,
And the fugitive moment refuses to stay:
The arrow is flown,
The moment is gone,
The millennial year
Rushes on to our view, and eternity's here.

3 O that each in the day
Of his coming, may say,
"I have fought my way through,
I have finished the work thou didst give me to do!"
O that each from his Lord
May receive the glad word,
"Well and faithfully done;
Enter into my joy, and sit down on my throne!"

107

"I am a stranger and a sojourner, as all my fathers were." Ps. xxxix. 12.

I'M a pilgrim, and I'm a stranger;
I can tarry but a night;
Do not detain me, for I am going
To where the rivers are ever flowing.

2 There the sunbeams are ever shining,
I am longing for the sight;
Within a country unknown and dreary,
I have been wandering, forlorn and weary.

3 Of the country to which I'm going,
My Redeemer is the light;
There is no sorrow, nor any sighing,
Nor any sinning, nor any dying.
I'm a pilgrim, and I'm a stranger,
I can tarry but a night.

108 7 s.

"Lovest thou me?" JOHN xxi. 16.

HARK, my soul! it is the Lord,—
'Tis thy Saviour, hear his word;
Jesus speaks, and speaks to thee;
"Say, poor sinner, lovest thou me?

2 "I delivered thee when bound,
And when wounded, healed thy wound;
Sought thee wandering, set thee right,
Turned thy darkness into light.

3 "Mine is an unchanging love,
Higher than the heights above;
Deeper than the depths beneath,
Free and faithful, strong as death.

4 "Thou shalt see my glory soon,
When the work of grace is done;
Partner of my throne shalt be;
Say, poor sinner, lovest thou me?"

5 Lord, it is my chief complaint,
That my love is weak and faint;
Yet I love thee and adore;
O for grace to love thee more!

109

"Draw nigh unto God, and he will draw nigh unto you." JAMES iv. 8.

NEARER, my God, to thee,—
Nearer to thee!
E'en though it be a cross
That raiseth me;
Still all my song shall be,
Nearer, my God, to thee,
Nearer to thee!

2 Though like a wanderer,
The sun gone down,
Darkness comes over me,
My rest a stone,
Yet in my dreams I'd be
Nearer, my God, to thee,
Nearer to thee!

3 There let my way appear
Steps unto heaven;
All that thou sendest me
In mercy given;
Angels to beckon me
Nearer, my God, to thee,
Nearer to thee!

4 Then with my waking thoughts
Bright with thy praise,
Out of my stony griefs
Bethel I'll raise;
So by my woes to be
Nearer, my God, to thee,
Nearer to thee!

5 And when on joyful wing,
Cleaving the sky,
Sun, moon, and stars forgot,
Upward I fly;
Still all my song shall be,
Nearer, my God, to thee,
Nearer to thee!

110 8, 7.

"Whosoever doth not bear his cross and come after me, cannot be my disciple." LUKE xiv. 27.

JESUS, I my cross have taken,
All to leave, and follow thee:
Naked, poor, despised, forsaken,
Thou, from hence, my all shalt be;
Perish every fond ambition,
All I've sought, or hoped, or known!
Yet how rich is my condition,
God and heaven are still my own!

2 Let the world despise and leave me;
They have left my Saviour, too;
Human hearts and looks deceive me,
Thou art not, like them, untrue;
O, while thou dost smile upon me,
God of wisdom, love, and might!
Foes may hate, and friends disown me,
Show thy face, and all is bright.

3 Perish, earthly fame and treasure!
Come, disaster, scorn, and pain!
In thy service, pain is pleasure;
With thy favour, life is gain:

O! 'tis not in grief to harm me,
While thy love is left to me;
O! 'twere not in joy to charm me—
Were that joy unmixed with thee.

111

"Christ in you, the hope of glory." COL. i. 27.

HOW happy are they
Who the Saviour obey,
And have laid up their treasure above!
O, what tongue can express
The sweet comfort and peace
Of a soul in its earliest love!

2 'Twas heaven below
My Redeemer to know,
And the angels could do nothing more
Than to fall at his feet,
And the story repeat,
And the lover of sinners adore.

3 Then, all the day long,
Was my Jesus my song,
And redemption through faith in his name:
O, that all might believe,
And salvation receive,
And their song and their joy be the same.

112 S. M.

"It is God which worketh in you both to will and to do of his good pleasure." PHIL. ii. 13.

HEIRS of unending life,
While yet we sojourn here,
O let us our salvation work
With trembling and with fear.

2 God will support our hearts
With might before unknown;
The work to be performed is ours,
The strength is all his own.

3 'Tis he that works to will,
'Tis he that works to do;
His is the power by which we act,
His be the glory too!

113 L. M.

"Forgetting those things which are behind."
PHIL. iii. 13.

FAREWELL, farewell to all below,
My Jesus calls, and I must go;
I launch my boat upon the sea,
This land is not the land for me.

2 I've found the winding path of sin
A rugged path to travel in;
Beyond the chilly waves I see
The land my Saviour bought for me.

3 Farewell, dear friends, I may not stay,
The home I seek is far away;
Where Christ is not, I cannot be;
This land is not the land for me.

4 My hope, my heart, is now on high,
There all my joys and treasures lie:
Where seraphs bow and bend the knee,
O, that's the land, the land for me.

114 C. M.

"I will give you rest." MATT. xi. 28.

I HEARD the voice of Jesus say,
Come unto me and rest:
Lay down, thou weary one, lay down
Thy head upon my breast.
I came to Jesus as I was,
Weary, and worn, and sad,
I found in him a resting place,
And he has made me glad.

2 I heard the voice of Jesus say,
Behold, I freely give
The living water; thirsty one,
Stoop down and drink and live.
I came to Jesus, and I drank
Of that life giving stream;
My thirst was quenched, my soul revived,
And now I live in him.

3 I heard the voice of Jesus say,
I am this dark world's light,
Look unto me, thy morn shall rise
And all thy day be bright.
I looked to Jesus, and I found
In him my Star, my Sun;
And in that light of life I'll walk,
Till travelling days are done.

115 7, 6.

"Jesus, the author and finisher of our faith."
HEB. xii. 2.

GOD of my salvation, hear,
And help me to believe;
Now to thee do I draw near,
Thy blessing to receive;
Full of sin, alas, I am,
But to thee for refuge flee;
Friend of sinners, spotless Lamb,
Thy blood was shed for me.

2 No good word, or work, or thought
I bring to buy thy grace;
Pardon I accept, unbought;
Thy proffer I embrace.
Needy, guilty, vile I am,
Yet I know thy love is free;
Friend of sinners, spotless Lamb,
Thy blood was shed for me.

3 Saviour, from thy wounded side
I never will depart;
At thy cross will I abide,
With humble, trusting heart;
When my place above I claim,
Still the cross shall be my plea;
Friend of sinners, spotless Lamb
Thy blood was shed for me.

116 S. M.

"Let us not sleep, as do others, but let us watch and be sober." 1 THESS. v. 6.

MY soul, be on thy guard,
 Ten thousand foes arise;
And hosts of sin are pressing hard,
 To draw thee from the skies.

2 O watch, and fight, and pray,
 The battle ne'er give o'er;
Renew it boldly every day,
 And help divine implore.

3 Ne'er think the victory won,
 Nor once at ease sit down;
Thine arduous work will not be done,
 Till thou hast got thy crown.

117 7, 6.

"There remaineth yet a rest to the people of God." HEB. iv. 9.

FROM every earthly pleasure,
 From every transient joy,
From every mortal treasure
 That soon will fade and die;
No longer these desiring,
 Upward our wishes tend,
To nobler bliss aspiring,
 And joys that never end.

2 From every piercing sorrow
 That heaves our breast to-day,
Or threatens us to-morrow,
 Hope turns our eyes away;

On wings of faith ascending,
  We see the land of light,
And feel our sorrows ending
  In infinite delight.

3 'Tis true we are but strangers
  And pilgrims here below,
And countless snares and dangers
  Surround the path we go:
Though painful and distressing,
  Yet there's a rest above;
And onward still we're pressing,
  To reach that land of love.

118 C. M.

"If we suffer, we shall also reign with him."
2 TIM. ii. 12.

MUST Jesus bear the cross alone,
  And all the world go free?
No, there's a cross for every one,
  And there's a cross for me.

2 The consecrated cross I'll bear,
  Till death shall set me free,
And then go home my crown to wear,
  For there's a crown for me.

---

3 Upon the crystal pavement, down
  At Jesus' pierced feet,
Joyful, I'll cast my golden crown,
  And his dear name repeat.

4 And palms shall wave, and harps shall ring
Beneath heaven's arches high,
The Lord that lives, the ransomed sing,
That lives no more to die.

5 O precious cross! O glorious crown!
O resurrection day!
Ye angels, from the stars come down,
And bear my soul away.

119 L. M.

"I go to prepare a place for you." JOHN xiv. 2.

AND art thou, gracious Master, gone,
A mansion to prepare for me?
Shall I behold thee on thy throne,
And there forever dwell with thee?
Then, let the world approve or blame,
I'll triumph in thy glorious name.

2 What transport, Lord, shall fill my heart,
When thou my worthless name shalt own!
When I shall see thee as thou art,
And know, as I myself am known!
From sin, and fear, and sorrow free,
My soul shall find its rest in thee.

120 7 S.

"Salvation to our God which sitteth upon the throne, and unto the Lamb." REV. vii. 10.

PALMS of glory, raiment bright,
Crowns that never fade away,
Gird and deck the saints in light,
Priests, and kings, and conquerors they.

2 Yet the conquerors bring their palms
To the Lamb amidst the throne,
And proclaim in joyful psalms,
Victory through his cross alone.

3 Kings for harps their crowns resign,
Crying, as they strike the chords,
"Take the kingdom, it is thine,
King of kings, and Lord of lords!"

4 Round the altar, priests confess,
If their robes are white as snow,
'Twas the Saviour's righteousness,
And his blood that made them so.

5 Who are these?—on earth they dwelt
Sinners once of Adam's race;
Guilt and fear and suffering felt,
But were saved by sovereign grace.

6 They were mortal, too, like us:
Ah! when we, like them, shall die,
May our souls, translated thus,
Triumph, reign, and shine on high.

121

"Here have we no continuing city, but we seek one to come." HEB. xiii. 14.

ONE sweetly solemn thought
Comes to me o'er and o'er;
I'm nearer my home to-day
Than I've ever been before.

2 Nearer my Father's house,
Where the many mansions be;
Nearer the great white throne,
Nearer the jasper sea:

3 Nearer the bound of life,
Where we lay our burdens down;
Nearer leaving my cross,
Nearer wearing my crown.

4 But lying darkly between,
Winding down through the night,
Is that dim and unknown stream
Which leads at last to light.

5 Father, perfect my trust,
Strengthen my feeble faith;
Let me feel as if I trod
The shore of the river death.

6 For even now my feet
May stand upon its brink,—
I may be nearer my home,
Nearer now than I think.

122

"We rejoice in the hope of the glory of God."
ROMANS v. 2.

MY days are gliding swiftly by,
And I, a pilgrim stranger,
Would not detain them as they fly,
Those hours of toil and danger.

2 We'll gird our loins, my brethren dear,
Our heavenly home discerning;
Our absent Lord has left us word,
Let every lamp be burning.

3 Should coming days be cold and dark,
We need not cease our singing;
That perfect rest naught can molest,
Where golden harps are ringing.

4 Let sorrow's rudest tempest blow,
Each chord on earth to sever;
Our King says come, and there's our home,
Forever, O forever!

CHORUS.

For O! we stand on Jordan's strand,
Our friends are passing over,
And just before, the shining shore
We may almost discover.

123 C. M.

"A better country, that is, an heavenly." HEB. xi. 16.

HOW pleasant thus to dwell below,
In fellowship of love;
And though we part, 'tis bliss to know
The good shall meet above.

2 Yes, happy thought! when we are free
From earthly grief and pain,
In heaven we shall each other see,
And never part again.

3 Then let us each, in strength divine,
Still walk in wisdom's ways;
That we, with those we love, may join
In never ending praise.

CHORUS.

O that will be joyful
To meet to part no more,
On Canaan's happy shore,
And sing the everlasting song,
With those who've gone before.

124 S. M.

"And so shall we ever be with the Lord."
1 THESS. iv. 17.

FOREVER with the Lord!
Amen, so let it be;
Life from the dead is in that word,
'Tis immortality.

2 Here in the body pent,
Absent from him I roam,
Yet nightly pitch my moving tent
A day's march nearer home.

3 My Father's house on high,
Home of my soul, how near
At times to Faith's illumined eye
Thy golden gates appear!

4 My thirsty spirit faints
To reach the land I love,
The bright inheritance of saints,
Jerusalem above.

125 C. M.

"An inheritance incorruptible, undefiled, and that fadeth not away." 1 PETER i. 4.

JERUSALEM, my happy home,
Name ever dear to me,
When shall my labours have an end,
In joy, and peace, and thee?

2 O when, thou city of my God,
Shall I thy courts ascend;
Where congregations ne'er break up,
And Sabbaths have no end?

3 There happier bowers than Eden's bloom,
Nor sin, nor sorrow know;
Blest seats! through rude and stormy scenes,
I onward press to you.

4 Why should I shrink at pain and woe,
Or feel at death dismay?
I've Canaan's goodly land in view,
And realms of endless day.

5 Apostles, martyrs, prophets, there
Around my Saviour stand;
And soon my friends in Christ below
Will join the glorious band.

6 Jerusalem, my happy home!
My soul still pants for thee;
Then shall my labours have an end,
When I thy joys shall see.

126

"O death, where is thy sting? O grave, where is thy victory?" 1 COR. xv. 55.

JOYFULLY, joyfully onward I move,
Bound to the land of bright spirits above;
Angelic choristers sing as I come,
Joyfully, joyfully haste to thy home!
Soon with my pilgrimage ended below,
Home to the land of bright spirits I go;
Pilgrim and stranger no more shall I roam,
Joyfully, joyfully resting at home.

2 Friends, fondly cherished, have passed on before;
Waiting, they watch me approaching the shore;
Singing to cheer me through death's chilling gloom,
Joyfully, joyfully haste to thy home.
Sounds of sweet melody fall on my ear;
Harps of the blessed, your voices I hear!
Rings with the harmony heaven's high dome,—
Joyfully, joyfully haste to thy home.

3 Death, with thy weapons of war lay me low,
Strike, king of terrors, I fear not the blow;
Jesus hath broken the bars of the tomb!

Joyfully, joyfully will I go home.
Bright will the morn of eternity dawn,
Death shall be banished, his sceptre be
    gone;
Joyfully, then, shall I witness his doom,
Joyfully, joyfully, safely at home.

127 7, 6.

"The world passeth away, and the lust thereof, but he that doeth the will of God abideth forever." 1 John ii. 17.

RISE, my soul, and stretch thy wings,
  Thy better portion trace;
Rise from transitory things
  Towards heaven, thy native place;
Sun, and moon, and stars decay,
  Time shall soon this earth remove;
Rise, my soul, and haste away
  To seats prepared above.

2 Rivers to the ocean run,
  Nor stay in all their course;
Fire, ascending, seeks the sun,
  Both speed them to their source:
So the soul that's born of God
  Pants to see his glorious face,
Upward tends to his abode,
  To rest in his embrace.

3 Cease, ye pilgrims, cease to mourn;
  Press onward to the prize;
Soon our Saviour will return,
  Triumphant, in the skies:

Yet a season, and you know
  Happy entrance will be given;
All our sorrows left below,
  And earth exchanged for heaven.

128 C. M.

"Now we see through a glass darkly; but then face to face." 1 Cor. xiii. 12.

COME, Lord, and warm each languid heart,
  Inspire each lifeless tongue;
And let the joys of heaven impart
  Their influence to our song.

2 Sorrow, and pain, and every care,
  And discord there shall cease;
And perfect joy and love sincere,
  Adorn the realms of peace.

3 The soul from sin forever free,
  Shall mourn its power no more;
But, clothed in spotless purity,
  Redeeming love adore.

4 There, on a throne (how dazzling bright!)
  The exalted Saviour shines;
And beams ineffable delight
  On all the heavenly minds.

5 There shall the followers of the Lamb
  Join in immortal songs;
And endless honours to his Name
  Employ their tuneful tongues.

6 Lord, tune our hearts to praise and love,
Our feeble notes inspire;
Till, in thy blissful courts above,
We join the angelic choir.

129 11 s.

"I would not live alway." Job vii. 16.

I WOULD not live alway: I ask not to stay
Where storm after storm rises dark o'er the way;
The few lurid mornings that dawn on us here
Are enough for life's woes, full enough for its cheer.

2 I would not live alway, thus fettered by sin,
Temptation without, and corruption within;
E'en the rapture of pardon is mingled with fears,
And the cup of thanksgiving with penitent tears.

3 I would not live alway; no, welcome the tomb;
Since Jesus hath lain there, I dread not its gloom:
There, sweet be my rest, till he bid me arise,
To hail him in triumph descending the skies.

4 Who, who would live alway, away from his God;
Away from yon heaven, that blissful abode;
Where the rivers of pleasure flow o'er the bright plains,
And the noontide of glory eternally reigns.

5 Where the saints of all ages in harmony meet,
Their Saviour and brethren transported to greet;
While the anthems of rapture unceasingly roll,
And the smile of the Lord is the feast of the soul!

130 8, 7, 4.

"Thou shalt guide me with thy counsel, and afterward receive me into glory." Ps. lxxiii. 24.

GUIDE me, O thou great Jehovah!
Pilgrim through this barren land;
I am weak, but thou art mighty,
Hold me with thy powerful hand:
Bread of heaven!
Feed me now and evermore.

2 Open now the crystal fountain,
Whence the healing waters flow;
Let the fiery, cloudy pillar,
Lead me all my journey through:
Strong Deliverer,
Be thou still my strength and shield.

3 When I tread the verge of Jordan,
Bid my anxious fears subside:
Thou of death and hell the conqueror,
Land me safe on Canaan's side:
Songs of praises
I will ever give to thee.

131 C. M.

PSALM XXIII.

THE Lord's my Shepherd, I'll not want,
He makes me down to lie,
In pastures green: he leadeth me
The quiet waters by.

2 My soul he doth restore again;
And me to walk doth make
Within the paths of righteousness,
Even for his own name's sake.

3 Yea, though I walk in death's dark vale,
Yet will I fear none ill;
For thou art with me, and thy rod
And staff me comfort still.

4 My table thou hast furnished
In presence of my foes;
My head thou dost with oil anoint,
And my cup overflows.

5 Goodness and mercy all my life
Shall surely follow me;
And in God's house forevermore
My dwelling place shall be.

132 C. M.

PSALM XXXIV.

THROUGH all the changing scenes of life,
  In trouble and in joy,
The praises of my God shall still
  My heart and tongue employ.

2 Of his deliverance I will boast
  Till all who are distrest,
From my example, comfort take,
  And charm their griefs to rest.

3 O, make but trial of his love,
  Experience will decide,
How blest are they, and only they,
  Who in his truth confide.

4 Fear him, ye saints, and you will then
  Have nothing else to fear:
Come, make his service your delight,
  He'll make your wants his care.

133 C. M.

PSALM XL.

I WAITED for the Lord my God
  And patiently did bear;
At length to me he did incline
  My voice and cry to hear.

2 He took me from a fearful pit,
  And from the miry clay,
And on a rock he set my feet,
  Establishing my way.

3 He put a new song in my mouth,
Our God to magnify:
Many shall see it, and shall fear,
And on the Lord rely.

4 O blessed is the man whose trust
Upon the Lord relies;
Respecting not the proud nor such
As turn aside to lies.

134 C. M.

PSALM XLIII.

O SEND thy light forth, and thy truth;
Let them be guides to me;
And bring me to thy holy hill,
Even where thy dwellings be.

2 Then will I to God's altar go,
To God, my chiefest joy;
Yea, God, my God, thy name to praise,
My harp I will employ.

3 Why art thou then cast down, my soul?
What should discourage thee?
And why with vexing thoughts art thou
Disquieted in me?

4 Still trust in God; for him to praise
Good cause I yet shall have;
He of my countenance is the health,
My God that doth me save.

135 S. M.

PSALM LXVII.

LORD, bless and pity us,
Shine on us with thy face:
That th' earth thy way, and nations all
May know thy saving grace.

2 Let people praise thee, Lord;
Let people all thee praise.
O let the nations all be glad,
In songs their voices raise:

3 Thou'lt justly people judge,
On earth rule nations all.
Let people praise thee, Lord; let them
Praise thee, both great and small.

4 The earth her fruit shall yield;
Our God shall blessing send.
God shall us bless; men shall him fear,
Unto earth's utmost end.

136 C. M.

PSALM LXXII.

THE city shall be flourishing,
Her citizens abound
In number shall, like to the grass
That grows upon the ground.

2 His name forever shall endure;
Last like the sun it shall:
Men shall be blessed in him, and blessed
All nations shall him call.

3 Now blessed be the Lord our God,
The God of Israel,
For he alone doth wondrous works,
In glory that excel.

4 And blessed be his glorious name
To all eternity;
The whole earth let his glory fill,
Amen, so let it be.

137 C. M.

PSALM LXXXIX.

O GREATLY blessed the people are
The joyful sound that know;
In brightness of thy face, O Lord,
They ever on shall go.

2 They in thy name shall all the day
Rejoice exceedingly;
And in thy righteousness shall they
Exalted be on high.

3 Because the glory of their strength
Doth only stand in thee;
And in thy favour shall our horn
And power exalted be.

4 For God is our defence; and he
To us doth safety bring;
The holy One of Israel
Is our almighty King.

138 C. M.

PSALM XCV.

O COME, let us sing to the Lord:
Come, let us every one,
A joyful noise make to the Rock
Of our salvation.

2 Let us before his presence come
With praise and thankful voice;
Let us sing psalms to him with grace,
And make a joyful noise.

3 For God, a great God, and great King,
Above all gods he is.
Depths of the earth are in his hand,
The strength of hills is his.

4 To him the spacious sea belongs,
For he the same did make;
The dry land also from his hands
Its form at first did take.

139 L. M.

PSALM C.

ALL people that on earth do dwell,
Sing to the Lord with cheerful voice,
Him serve with mirth, his praise forth tell,
Come ye before him and rejoice.

2 Know that the Lord is God indeed;
Without our aid he did us make:
We are his flock, he doth us feed,
And for his sheep he doth us take.

3 O enter, then, his gates with praise,
Approach with joy his courts unto;
Praise, laud, and bless his name always,
For it is seemly so to do.

4 For why? the Lord our God is good,
His mercy is forever sure;
His truth at all times firmly stood
And shall from age to age endure.

140 L. M.

PSALM CII.

THOU shalt arise, and mercy yet
Thou to mount Sion shalt extend;
Her time for favour which was set,
Behold, is now come to an end.

2 Thy saints take pleasure in her stones:
Her very dust to them is dear,
All heathen lands and kingly thrones,
On earth thy glorious name shall fear.

3 God in his glory shall appear,
When Sion he builds and repairs,
He shall regard and lend his ear
Unto the needy's humble prayers.

4 Th' afflicted's prayer he will not scorn.
All times this shall be on record:
And generations yet unborn
Shall praise and magnify the Lord.

141 S. M.

PSALM CIII.

O THOU, my soul, bless God the Lord,
And all that in me is,
Be stirred up, his holy name
To magnify and bless.

2 Bless, O my soul, the Lord thy God;
And not forgetful be
Of all his gracious benefits
He hath bestowed on thee.

3 All thine iniquities who doth
Most graciously forgive:
Who thy diseases all and pains
Doth heal and thee relieve:

4 Who doth redeem thy life, that thou
To death may'st not go down;
Who thee with loving kindness doth
And tender mercies crown.

142 L. M.

PSALM CXLV.

O LORD, thou art my God and King:
Thee will I magnify and praise;
I will thee bless, and gladly sing
Unto thy holy name always.

2 Each day I rise I will thee bless,
And praise thy name time without end.
Much to be praised and great God is;
His greatness none can comprehend.

3 Race shall thy works praise unto race,
The mighty acts show done by thee;
I will speak of thy glorious grace,
And honour of thy majesty.

4 Thy wondrous works I will record,
By men the might shall be extolled
Of all thy dreadful acts, O Lord,
And I thy greatness will unfold.

143 H. M.

PSALM CXLVIII.

THE Lord of heaven confess,
On high his glory raise;
Him let all angels bless;
Him all his armies praise.
Him glorify,
Sun, moon, and stars;
Ye higher spheres,
And cloudy sky.

2 O let God's name be praised
Above both earth and sky,
For he his saints hath raised,
And set their horn on high.
Even those that be
Of Israel's race,
Near to his grace,—
The Lord praise ye.

144 8, 7, 4.

"Save thy people and bless thine inheritance; feed them also, and lift them up forever." Ps. xxviii. 9.

LORD, dismiss us with thy blessing,
Fill our hearts with joy and peace;
Let us each thy love possessing,
Triumph in redeeming grace;
O refresh us,
Travelling through this wilderness.

2 Thanks we give, and adoration
For the gospel's joyful sound;
May the fruits of thy salvation
In our hearts and lives abound;
May thy presence
With us evermore be found.

3 So, whene'er the signal's given,
Us from earth to call away;
Borne on angels' wings to heaven,
Glad to leave our cumbrous clay,—
May we, ready,
Rise and reign in endless day.

145 L. M.

"Be perfectly joined together in the same mind." 1 Cor. i. 10.

COME, Christian brethren, ere we part,
Join every voice and every heart,
One solemn hymn to God we raise,
One final song of grateful praise.

2 Christians, we here may meet no more,
But there is yet a happier shore;
And there, released from toil and pain,
Dear brethren, we shall meet again.

146 L. M.

"He whom thou blessest is blessed." NUMB. xxii. 6.

DISMISS us with thy blessing, Lord,
Help us to feed upon thy word;
All that has been amiss, forgive,
And let thy truth within us live.

2 Though we are guilty, thou art good;
Wash all our works in Jesus' blood;
Give every fettered soul release,
And bid us all depart in peace.

147 L. M.

"The Father, the Word, and the Holy Ghost, and these three are one." 1 JOHN v. 7.

PRAISE God from whom all blessings flow;
Praise him, all creatures here below;
Praise him above, ye heavenly host,
Praise Father, Son, and Holy Ghost.

148 C. M.

"To whom be honour and power everlasting." 1 TIM. vi. 16.

NOW to the Lamb that once was slain,
Be endless blessings paid;
Salvation, glory, joy remain
Forever on thy head.

2 Thou hast redeemed us by thy blood,
And set the prisoners free;
Hast made us kings and priests to God,
And we shall reign with thee.

149 7, 6.

"I will yet praise thee more and more."
Ps. lxxi. 14.

ETERNAL praise be given,
And songs of highest worth,
By all the hosts of heaven,
And all the saints on earth,
To God, supreme confessed,
To Christ, his only Son,
And to the Spirit blessed,
Eternal Three in One.

150 8, 7, 4.

"Praise ye the Lord." Ps. cl. 1.

GREAT Jehovah, we adore thee,
God the Father, God the Son,
God the Spirit, joined in glory
On the same eternal throne:
Endless praises
To Jehovah, Three in One.

151 11 s.

"While I live will I praise the Lord; I will sing praises unto my God while I have any being." Ps. cxlvi. 2.

COME, let us adore him; come, bow at his feet;
O! give him the glory, the praise that is meet;

Let joyful hosannas unceasing arise,
And join the full chorus that gladdens the
skies.

152 8, 7.

"The grace of the Lord Jesus Christ, and the love of God, and the communion of the Holy Ghost be with you all. Amen." 2 COR. xiii. 14.

MAY the grace of Christ our Saviour,
And the Father's boundless love,
With the Holy Spirit's favour,
Rest upon us from above!
Thus may we abide in union
With each other and the Lord!
And possess, in sweet communion,
Joys which earth cannot afford.

153 8, 7, 4.

"Unto him that hath loved us, and washed us from our sins in his own blood, and hath made us kings and priests unto God and his Father; to him be glory and dominion forever and ever. Amen." REV. i. 5, 6.

NOW to him who loved us,—gave us
Every pledge that love could give,—
Freely shed his blood to save us,—
Gave his life that we might live,—
Be the kingdom,
And dominion,—
Glory be forevermore.

Additional Hymns.

154 H. M.

"Thine, O Lord, is the greatness, and the power, and the glory, and the victory, and the majesty."
1 CHRON. xxix. 11.

WE give immortal praise
To God the Father's love,
For all our comforts here,
And all our hopes above:
He sent his own
Eternal Son
To die for sins
That man had done.

2 To God the Son belongs
Immortal glory too,
Who saved us by his blood
From everlasting woe:
And now he lives,
And now he reigns,
And sees the fruit
Of all his pains.

3 To God the Spirit, praise
And endless worship give,
Whose new-creating power
Makes the dead sinner live:
His work completes
The great design,
And fills the soul
With joy divine.

4 Almighty God, to thee
Be endless honours done;
The Sacred Persons Three,
The Godhead only One;
Where reason fails
With all her powers,
There faith prevails,
And love adores.

155 8, 7.

"I have waited for thy salvation, O Lord."
GEN. xlix. 18.

HAIL! thou long expected Jesus,
Born to set thy people free:
From our sins and fears release us,
Let us find our rest in thee.

2 Israel's strength and consolation,
Hope of all the saints thou art;
Long desired of every nation,
Joy of every waiting heart.

3 Born thy people to deliver,
Born a child, yet God our King,
Born to reign in us forever,
Now thy gracious kingdom bring.

4 By thine own eternal Spirit,
Rule in all our hearts alone;
By thine all-sufficient merit,
Raise us to thy glorious throne.

156 L. M.

"God forbid that I should glory, save in the cross of our Lord Jesus Christ, by whom the world is crucified unto me, and I unto the world." GAL. vi. 14.

WHEN I survey the wondrous cross
On which the Prince of Glory died,
My richest gain I count but loss,
And pour contempt on all my pride.

2 Forbid it, Lord, that I should boast,
Save in the cross of Christ my God:
All the vain things that charm me most,
I sacrifice them to thy blood.

3 See! from his head, his hands, his feet,
Sorrow and love flow mingled down:
Did e'er such love and sorrow meet?
Or thorns compose a Saviour's crown?

4 Were the whole realm of nature mine,
That were a tribute far too small;
Love so amazing, so divine,
Demands my life, my soul, my all.

157 C. M.

"Not by works of righteousness which we have done, but according to his mercy he saved us." TITUS iii. 5.

MY grateful soul, forever praise,
Forever love his Name,
Who turned thee from the fatal paths
Of folly, sin, and shame.

2 Vain and presumptuous is the trust
Which in our works we place;
Salvation from a higher source
Flows to our fallen race.

3 'Tis from the love of God through Christ
That all our hopes begin;
His mercy saved our souls from death
And washed us from our sin.

4 His Spirit, through the Saviour shed,
His sacred fire imparts,
Removes our dross, and love divine
Enkindles in our hearts.

5 Thus raised from death we live anew;
And, justified by grace,
We hope in glory to appear,
And see our Father's face.

158

"Look unto me and be ye saved, all the ends of the earth." ISAIAH xlv. 22.

BY faith I view my Saviour dying
On the tree;
To every nation he is crying,
Look to me!
He bids the guilty now draw near,
Repent, believe, dismiss their fear;—
Hark! hark! what precious words I hear!
Mercy's free! Mercy's free!

2 Did Christ, when I was sin pursuing,
Pity me?
And did he snatch my soul from ruin?
Can it be?
O yes! he did salvation bring:
He is my Prophet, Priest, and King;
And now my happy soul can sing,—
Mercy's free! Mercy's free.

3 Jesus my weary soul refreshes;—
Mercy's free!
And every moment Christ is precious
Unto me.
None can describe the bliss I prove,
While through this wilderness I rove:
All may enjoy the Saviour's love,
Mercy's free! Mercy's free!

4 Long as I live, I'll still be crying,
"Mercy's free!"
And this shall be my theme when dying,
"Mercy's free!"
And when the vale of death I've passed,
When lodged above the stormy blast,
I'll sing, while endless ages last,
"Mercy's free! Mercy's free."

159 H. M.

"He is able to save them to the uttermost, that come unto God by him, seeing he ever liveth to make intercession for them." HEB. vii. 25.

ARISE, my soul, arise;
Shake off thy guilty fears;

The bleeding Sacrifice
In my behalf appears:
Before the throne my Surety stands,
My name is written on his hands.

2 He ever lives above,
For me to intercede;
His all-redeeming love,
His precious blood, to plead;
His blood atoned for all our race,
And sprinkles now the throne of grace.

160 L. M.

"I have loved thee with an everlasting love."
JER. xxxi. 3.

JESUS, I know, hath died for me,—
Here is my hope, my joy, my rest;
Hither, when hell assails, I flee,
And look into my Saviour's breast:
Away, sad doubts and anxious fear,
Mercy is all that's written there.

2 Though waves and storms go o'er my head,
Though strength, and health, and friends be gone;
Though joys be withered all, and dead,
And every comfort be withdrawn;
Steadfast on this my soul relies,
Father, thy mercy never dies.

3 Fixed on this rock will I remain,
When heart shall fail and flesh decay;

A rock which shall my soul sustain,
  When earth's foundations melt away:
Mercy's full power I then shall prove,
Loved with an everlasting love.

161

"The love of Christ, which passeth knowledge."
EPH. iii. 19.

HOW great is the love
  Which Jesus hath shown!
He came from above,
  From heaven's bright throne,
That he might deliver
  Poor sinners from hell,
And take them forever
  In glory to dwell.

162 C. M.

"I will sing praise unto thy name forever."
Ps. lxi. 8.

JESUS, I love thy charming name;
  'Tis music to my ear;
Fain would I sound it out so loud
  That earth and heaven might hear.

2 Yes,—thou art precious to my soul,
  My transport and my trust;
Jewels to thee are gaudy toys,
  And gold is sordid dust.

3 Thy grace shall dwell upon my heart,
  And shed its fragrance there;

The noblest balm of all its wounds,
  The cordial of its care.

4 I'll speak the honours of thy name
  With my last labouring breath;
Then, speechless, clasp thee in my arms,
  The antidote of death.

163 C. M.

"Unto you which believe, he is precious."
1 Pet. ii. 7.

HOW sweet the name of Jesus sounds
  In a believer's ear!
It soothes his sorrows, heals his wounds,
  And drives away his fear.

2 It makes the wounded spirit whole,
  And calms the troubled breast;
'Tis manna to the hungry soul,
  And to the weary, rest.

3 Weak is the effort of my heart,
  And cold my warmest thought;
But when I see thee as thou art,
  I'll praise thee as I ought.

CHORUS.

I do believe, I now believe,
  That Jesus died for me,
And through his blood, his precious blood,
  I shall from sin be free.

164 L. M.

"We have seen his star in the east." MATT. ii. 2.

WHEN marshalled on the nightly plain,
The glittering host bestud the sky;
One star alone, of all the train,
Can fix the sinner's wandering eye.

2 Hark! hark! to God the chorus breaks,
From every host, from every gem;
But one alone the Saviour speaks,
It is the Star of Bethlehem.

3 Once on the raging seas I rode,
The storm was loud, the night was dark;
The ocean yawned, and rudely blowed
The wind that tossed my foundering bark.

4 Deep horror then my vitals froze,
Death-struck, I ceased the tide to stem;
When suddenly a star arose,
It was the Star of Bethlehem!

5 It was my Guide, my Light, my All,
It bade my dark forebodings cease;
And, through the storm and danger's thrall,
It led me to the port of peace.

6 Now, safely moored, my perils o'er,
I'll sing, first in night's diadem,
Forever, and forevermore,
The Star, the Star of Bethlehem!

165 11, 10.

"And are come to worship him." MATT. ii. 2.

BRIGHTEST and best of the sons of the morning,
Dawn on our darkness and lend us thine aid!
Star of the East, the horizon adorning,
Guide where our infant Redeemer is laid.

2 Cold on his cradle the dewdrops are shining,
Low lies his head with the beasts of the stall;
Angels adore him in slumber reclining,
Maker, and Monarch, and Saviour of all.

3 Say, shall we yield him, in costly devotion,
Odours of Edom, and offerings divine?
Gems of the mountain, and pearls of the ocean,
Myrrh from the forest, or gold from the mine?

4 Vainly we offer each ample oblation;
Vainly with gifts would his favour secure;

Richer by far is the heart's adoration;
Dearer to God are the prayers of the poor.

CHORUS.

Hallelujah to the Lamb, who has purchased our pardon;
We'll praise him again when we pass over Jordan.

166 L. M.

"One thing is needful." LUKE x. 42.

JESUS, engrave it on my heart,
That thou the one thing needful art;
I could from all things parted be,
But never, never, Lord, from thee.

2 Needful is thy most precious blood;
Needful is thy correcting rod;
Needful is thy indulgent care;
Needful thy all prevailing prayer.

3 Needful thy presence, dearest Lord,
True peace and comfort to afford;
Needful thy promise to impart
Fresh life and vigour to my heart.

4 Needful art thou, my Guide, my Stay,
Through all life's dark and weary way;
Nor less in death thou'lt needful be,
To bring my spirit home to thee.

5 Then, needful still, my God, my King,
Thy name eternally I'll sing!
Glory and praise be ever HIS,
The one THING NEEDFUL JESUS IS!

167 L. M.

"Because I live, ye shall live also." JOHN xiv. 19.

IF my immortal Saviour lives,
Then my immortal life is sure:
His word a firm foundation gives;
Here I may build, and rest secure.

2 Here let my faith unshaken dwell;
Forever firm the promise stands:
Not all the powers of earth or hell
Can e'er dissolve the sacred bands.

3 Here, O my soul, thy trust repose:
If Jesus is forever mine,
Not death itself—that last of foes—
Shall break a union so divine.

168 L. M.

"And there I will meet thee, and I will commune with thee from above the mercy-seat." Ex. xxv. 22.

JESUS, where'er thy people meet,
There they behold thy mercy-seat;
Where'er they seek thee, thou art found;
And every place is hallowed ground.

2 Dear Shepherd of thy chosen few,
Thy former mercies here renew;

Here to our waiting hearts proclaim
The sweetness of thy saving name.

3 Here may we prove the power of prayer,
To strengthen faith and banish care;
To teach our faint desires to rise
To things unseen beyond the skies.

4 Lord, we are few, but thou art near;
Nor short thine arm, nor deaf thine ear;
O, rend the heavens this favoured hour,
Let us now feel thy saving power.

169

"Is any afflicted among you? Let him pray."
JAMES v. 13.

COME, ye disconsolate, where'er ye languish,
Come, at the mercy seat fervently kneel:
Here bring your wounded hearts, here tell your anguish;
Earth has no sorrow that heaven cannot heal.

2 Joy of the desolate, light of the straying,
Hope of the penitent, fadeless and pure,
Here speaks the Comforter, in mercy saying,
Earth has no sorrow that heaven cannot cure.

170 7 s.

" Where two or three are gathered together in my name, there am I in the midst of them."
MATT. xviii. 20.

SAVIOUR, at thy feet we bow ;
O vouchsafe to meet us now !
At thy people's earnest cry,
Bring thy loving mercy nigh.

2 Thou hast said, where two or three
In thy worship shall agree,
That thou wilt be present there,
Answering their faithful prayer.

3 Lord, we plead thy promise here,
Let thy presence now appear;
On our souls thy Spirit pour,
Light, and life, and peace restore.

4 Raise our thoughts from things below ;
Faith's discerning eye bestow ;
Let our hearts, from sin made free,
Hold sweet intercourse with thee.

5 With a beam of living fire
Purify each low desire ;
Be thou, Lord, our Aim and End,
Our best Hope, and dearest Friend.

171 7 s.

" Having the promise of the life which now is, and of that which is to come." 1 TIM. iv. 8.

IF 'tis sweet to mingle where
Christians meet for social prayer ;

If 'tis sweet with them to raise
Songs of holy joy and praise,—
Sweeter far that state must be
Where they meet eternally.

2 Saviour, may these meetings prove
Preparations for above;
While we worship in this place,
May we go from grace to grace;
Till we each, in his degree,
Fit for endless glory be.

172 L. M.

"Serve the Lord with gladness: come before his presence with singing." Ps. c. 1.

WITH one consent let all the earth
To God their cheerful voices raise;
Glad homage pay with awful mirth,
And sing before him songs of praise.

2 Convinced that he is God alone,
From whom both we and all proceed;
We, whom he chooses for his own,
The flock that he vouchsafes to feed.

3 O enter, then, his temple gate,
Thence to his courts devoutly press:
And still your grateful hymns repeat,
And still his Name with praises bless.

4 For he's the Lord, supremely good,
His mercy is forever sure:
His truth, which always firmly stood,
To endless ages shall endure.

173 7 s.

"Let us make a joyful noise unto the rock of our salvation." Ps. xcv. 1.

NOW begin the heavenly theme,
Sing aloud in Jesus' name;
Ye, who his salvation prove,
Triumph in redeeming love.

2 Ye, who see the Father's grace,
Beaming in the Saviour's face,
As to Canaan on ye move,
Praise and bless redeeming love.

3 Mourning souls, dry up your tears,
Banish all your guilty fears,
See your guilt and curse remove,
Cancelled by redeeming love.

4 Ye, alas! who long have been
Willing slaves of death and sin!
Now from bliss no longer rove,
Stop, and taste redeeming love.

5 Welcome, all by sin oppressed,
Welcome to his sacred rest:
Nothing brought him from above,
Nothing,—but redeeming love.

6 Hither, then, your music bring,
Strike aloud each joyful string;
Mortals, join the hosts above,
Join to praise redeeming love.

174

8, 7.

"Now thanks be to God which always causeth us to triumph in Christ." 2 COR. ii. 14.

LORD, with glowing heart I'd praise thee,
For the bliss thy love bestows;
For the pardoning grace that saves me,
And the peace that from it flows:
Help, O God, my weak endeavour;
This dull soul to rapture raise;
Thou must light the flame, or never
Can my love be warmed to praise.

2 Praise, my soul, the God that sought thee,
Wretched wanderer, far astray;
Found thee lost and kindly brought thee
From the paths of death away;
Praise, with love's devoutest feeling,
Him who saw thy guilt born fear,
And, the light of hope revealing,
Bade the blood stained cross appear.

3 Lord, this bosom's ardent feeling
Vainly would my lips express:
Low before thy footstool kneeling,
Deign thy suppliant's prayer to bless:
Let thy grace, my soul's chief treasure,
Love's pure flame within me raise;
And, since words can never measure,
Let my life show forth thy praise.

175 L. M.

"My soul shall be joyful in my God." ISAIAH lxi. 10.

ALL glorious God, what hymns of praise
Shall our transported voices raise:
What ardent love and zeal are due,
While heaven stands open to our view.

2 Once we were fallen, and O how low!
Just on the brink of endless woe;
When Jesus, from the realms above,
Borne on the wings of boundless love,

3 Scattered the shades of death and night,
And spread around his heavenly light:
By him what wondrous grace is shown
To souls impoverished and undone.

4 He shows, beyond these mortal shores,
A bright inheritance as ours;
Where saints in light our coming wait
To share their holy, happy state.

176 S. M.

"Bless the Lord, O my soul, and all that is within me, bless his holy name." Ps. ciii. 1.

O BLESS the Lord, my soul,
His grace to thee proclaim;
And all that is within me, join
To bless his holy Name.

2 O bless the Lord, my soul,
His mercies bear in mind;

Forget not all his benefits,
Who is to thee so kind.

3 He pardons all thy sins,
Prolongs thy feeble breath;
He healeth thine infirmities,
And ransoms thee from death.

4 He feeds thee with his love,
Upholds thee with his truth;
And, like the eagle's, he renews
The vigour of thy youth.

5 Then bless the Lord, my soul,
His grace, his love proclaim;
Let all that is within me, join
To bless his holy Name.

177

7 s.

"Turn ye, turn ye from your evil ways; for why will ye die?" EZEK. xxxiii. 11.

SINNERS, turn, why will ye die?
God, your Maker, asks you why:
God, who did your being give,
Made you with himself to live,
He the fatal cause demands,
Asks the work of his own hands:
Why, ye thankless creatures, why
Will ye cross his love, and die?

2 Sinners, turn, why will ye die?
God, your Saviour, asks you why;

He, who did your souls retrieve,
Died himself that ye might live,
Will you let him die in vain?
Crucify your Lord again?
Why, ye ransomed sinners, why
Will ye slight his grace and die?

3 Sinners, turn, why will ye die?
God, the Spirit, asks you why?
He who all your lives hath strove,
Wooed you to embrace his love,
Will ye not his grace receive?
Will ye still refuse to live?
O, ye dying sinners, why,
Why will ye forever die?

178 S. M.

"Behold, now is the accepted time; behold, now is the day of salvation." 1 COR. vi. 2.

NOW is the accepted time,
Now is the day of grace;
Now, sinners, come without delay,
And seek the Saviour's face.

2 Now is the accepted time,
The Saviour calls to day;
To-morrow it may be too late,—
Then why should you delay?

3 Now is the accepted time,
The Gospel bids you come;
And every promise in his word
Declares there yet is room.

4 Lord, draw reluctant souls,
And feast them with thy love;
Then will the angels swiftly fly,
And bear the news above.

179 C. M.

"He shall call upon me, and I WILL answer him."
Ps. xci. 15.

COME, trembling sinner, in whose breast
A thousand thoughts revolve;
Come, with your guilt and fear oppressed,
And make this last resolve:

2 I'll go to Jesus, though my sin
Hath like a mountain rose;
I know his courts, I'll enter in,
Whatever may oppose.

3 Perhaps he will admit my plea,
Perhaps will hear my prayer;
But if I perish, I will pray,
And perish only there.

4 I can but perish if I go;
I am resolved to try;
For if I stay away, I know
I must forever die.

180

"He that hath ears to hear, let him hear."
MARK iv. 9.

TO-DAY the Saviour calls,
Ye wanderers, come!
O, ye benighted souls,
Why longer roam?

2 To-day the Saviour calls!
For refuge fly;
The storm of vengeance falls,
Ruin is nigh.

3 To-day the Saviour calls!
O, listen now!
Within these sacred walls
To Jesus bow.

4 The Spirit calls to-day!
Yield to his power;
O, grieve him not away!
'Tis mercy's hour.

181 L. M.

"Shall thy loving kindness be declared in the grave?"
Ps. lxxxviii. 11.

WHILE life prolongs its precious light,
Mercy is found, and peace is given;
But soon, ah! soon, approaching night
Shall blot out every hope of heaven.

2 Soon, born on time's most rapid wing,
Shall death command you to the grave,
Before his bar your spirits bring,
And none be found to hear or save.

3 In that lone land of deep despair
No Sabbath's heavenly light shall rise,
No God regard your bitter prayer,
No Saviour call you to the skies.

4 While God invites, how blest the day!
How sweet the gospel's charming sound!
Come sinners, haste, O, haste away,
While yet a pardoning God is found.

182 S. M.

"We shall all stand before the judgment seat of Christ." ROMANS xiv. 10.

AND will the Judge descend?
And must the dead arise?
And not a single soul escape
His all discerning eyes?

2 How will my heart endure
The terrors of that day,
When earth and heaven before his face
Astonished shrink away?

3 But ere the trumpet shakes
The mansions of the dead,
Hark! from the Gospel's cheering sound,
What joyful tidings spread.

4 Ye sinners, seek his grace,
Whose wrath ye cannot bear;
Fly to the shelter of his cross,
And find salvation there.

183 S. M.

"We, being many, are one body in Christ, and every one members one of another." ROMANS xii. 5.

BLEST be the tie that binds
Our hearts in Christian love;
The fellowship of kindred minds
Is like to that above.

2 Before our Father's throne,
We pour our ardent prayers;
Our fears, our hopes, our aims are one,
Our comforts and our cares.

3 We share our mutual woes,
Our mutual burdens bear;
And often, for each other, flows
The sympathizing tear.

4 When we asunder part,
It gives us inward pain;
But we shall still be joined in heart,
And hope to meet again.

5 From sorrow, toil, and pain,
And sin, we shall be free;
And perfect love and friendship reign,
Through all eternity.

184 L. M.

"Teach me thy way, O Lord; I will walk in thy truth." Ps. lxxxvi. 11.

MY God, permit me not to be
A stranger to myself and thee;
Amidst a thousand thoughts I rove,
Forgetful of my highest love.

2 Why should my passions mix with earth,
And thus debase my heavenly birth?
Why should I cleave to things below,
And all my purest joys forego?

3 Call me away from flesh and sense;
Thy grace, O Lord, can draw me thence:
I would obey thy voice divine,
And all inferior joys resign.

185 L. M.

"Thus saith the Lord of hosts; Consider your ways"
HAGGAI i. 5.

AS o'er the past my memory strays,
Why heaves the secret sigh?
'Tis that I mourn departed days,
Still unprepared to die.

2 The world and worldly things beloved,
My anxious thoughts employed;
And time unhallowed, unimproved,
Presents a fearful void.

3 Yet, holy Father, wild despair
Chase from my labouring breast;
Thy grace it is which prompts the prayer,
That grace can do the rest.

4 My life's brief remnant all be thine,
And when thy sure decree
Bids me this fleeting breath resign,
O speed my soul to thee.

186 C. M.

"Our light affliction, which is but for a moment, work eth for us a far more exceeding and eternal weight of glory." 2 COR. iv. 17.

WE seek a rest beyond the skies,
In everlasting day;

Through floods and flames the passage lies,
But Jesus guards the way.

2 The swelling flood and raging flame
Hear and obey his word;
Then let us triumph in his name,
Our Saviour is the Lord.

187 7 s.

"Jesus Christ came into the world to save sinners; of whom I am chief." 1 TIM. i. 15.

SOVEREIGN Ruler, Lord of all,
Prostrate at thy feet I fall:
Hear, O hear my earnest cry:
Frown not, lest I faint and die.

2 Vilest of the sons of men,
Chief of sinners, I have been;
Oft have sinned before thy face;
Trampled on thy richest grace.

3 Justly might thy fatal dart
Pierce this guilty, broken heart;
Justly might thy righteous breath
Doom me to eternal death.

4 Jesus, save my dying soul;
Make my broken spirit whole;
Humbled in the dust I lie;
Saviour, leave me not to die.

188

6, 4.

"In thee, O Lord, do I put my trust; let me never be put to confusion." Ps. lxxi. 1.

MY faith looks up to thee,
Thou Lamb of Calvary,
Saviour divine!
Now hear me while I pray,
Take all my guilt away,
O let me from this day
Be wholly thine.

2 May thy rich grace impart
Strength to my fainting heart;
My zeal inspire:
As thou hast died for me,
O may my love to thee,
Pure, warm, and changeless be,
A living fire.

3 While life's dark maze I tread,
And griefs around me spread,
Be thou my Guide:
Bid darkness turn to day,
Wipe sorrow's tears away,
Nor let me ever stray
From thee aside.

4 When ends life's transient dream,
When death's cold, sullen stream
Shall o'er me roll,
Blest Saviour, then in love,
Fear and distrust remove:
O bear me safe above,
A ransomed soul.

189 7 s.

"The sufferings of this present time are not worthy to be compared with the glory which shall be revealed in us." ROMANS viii. 18.

BRETHREN, while we sojourn here,
Fight we must, but should not fear;
Foes we have, but we've a Friend,
One that loves us to the end:
Forward, then, with courage go,
Long we shall not dwell below;
Soon the joyful news will come,
"Child, your Father calls, Come home."

2 In the way a thousand snares
Lie to take us unawares;
Satan, with malicious art,
Watches each unguarded heart:
But from Satan's malice free,
Saints shall soon in glory be;
Soon the joyful news will come,
"Child, your Father calls, Come home."

190 C. M.

"In the world ye shall have tribulation; but be of good cheer; I have overcome the world." JOHN xvi. 33.

'TIS my happiness below
Not to live without the cross;
But the Saviour's power to know,
Sanctifying every loss.

2 Trials must and will befall;
But with humble faith to see

Love inscribed upon them all,
This is happiness to me.

3 Did I meet no trials here,
No chastisement by the way,
Might I not with reason fear
I should be a cast-away ?

4 Trials make the promise sweet;
Trials give new life to prayer;
Bring me to my Saviour's feet,
Lay me low, and keep me there.

191 C. M.

"As in Adam all die, even so in Christ shall all be made alive." 1 COR. xv. 22.

HOW helpless guilty nature lies,
Unconscious of its load:
The heart unchanged can never rise
To happiness and God.

2 Can aught beneath a power divine
The stubborn will subdue?
'Tis thine, Almighty Saviour, thine
To form the heart anew.

3 'Tis thine the passions to recall
And upwards bid them rise;
And make the scales of error fall
From reason's darkened eyes.

4 To chase the shades of death away,
And bid the sinner live,
A beam of heaven, a vital ray,
'Tis thine alone to give.

5 O change these wretched hearts of ours,
   And give them life divine;
 Then shall our passions and our powers,
   Almighty Lord, be thine.

192 C. M.

"Every good and perfect gift is from above."
JAMES i. 17.

FATHER, to thee my soul I lift,
   On thee my hope depends,
 Convinced that every perfect gift
   From thee alone descends.

2 Mercy and grace are thine alone,
   And power and wisdom too;
 Without the Spirit of thy Son
   We nothing good can do.

3 Thou all our works in us hast wrought,
   Our good is all divine;
 The praise of every holy thought
   And righteous word is thine.

4 From thee, through Jesus, we receive
   The power on thee to call,
 In whom we are, and move, and live:
   Our God is all in all.

193 L. M.

"Thou canst make me clean." MARK i. 40.

O, THAT my load of sin were gone,
   O, that I could at last submit
 At Jesus' feet to lay it down,
   To lay my soul at Jesus' feet!

2 Rest for my soul I long to find;
  Saviour of all, if mine thou art,
Give me thy meek and lowly mind,
  And stamp thine image on my heart.

3 Break off the yoke of inbred sin,
  And fully set my spirit free;
I cannot rest till pure within,
  Till I am wholly lost in thee.

4 Fain would I learn of thee, my God;
  Thy light and easy burden prove,
The cross, all stained with hallowed blood,
  The labour of thy dying love.

5 I would, but thou must give the power,
  My heart from every sin release;
Bring near, bring near the joyful hour,
  And fill me with thy perfect peace.

194 S. M.

"Awake, thou that sleepest, and arise from the dead, and Christ shall give thee light." EPH. V. 14.

AH! when shall I awake
  From sin's soft soothing power;
The slumber from my spirit shake,
  And rise to fall no more?
Awake, no more to sleep,
  But stand with constant care,
Look up to God my soul to keep,
  And ever watch in prayer.

2 O, could I always pray,
  And never, never faint,
Freely to God might I convey
  Each woe and each complaint;
Before him might I lie,
  And tell him all my care;
And "Father, Abba, Father," cry,
  And pour a ceaseless prayer.

3 My Saviour, I would wait
  Till thou shalt make me whole;
Till thou shalt all things new create
  In my believing soul;
Till thou my sins subdue,
  Till thou my sins destroy,
My spirit after God renew,
  And fill with peace and joy.

195 10 s.

"Abide with us; for it is toward evening, and the day is far spent." LUKE xxiv. 29.

ABIDE with me; fast falls the eventide;
The darkness thickens. Lord, with me abide;
When other helpers fail, and comforts flee,
Help of the helpless, O abide with me.

2 Swift to its close ebbs out life's little day;
Earth's joys grow dim, its glories pass away;
Change and decay in all around I see,—
O thou who changest not, abide with me.

3 I need thy presence every passing hour;
What but thy grace can foil the tempter's power?
Who like thyself my guide and stay can be?
Through cloud and sunshine, O abide with me.

4 I fear no foe with thee at hand to bless;
Ills have no weight, and tears no bitterness.
Where is Death's sting? Where, Grave, thy victory?
I triumph still, if thou abide with me.

196 C. M.

"The Lord is at hand." PHIL. iv. 5.

TIME hastens on: ye longing saints,
Now raise your voices high;
And magnify that sovereign love
Which shows salvation nigh.

2 As time departs salvation comes;
Each moment brings it near;
Then welcome each declining day,
Welcome each closing year.

3 Not many years their course shall run,
Not many mornings rise,
Ere all its glories stand revealed
To our transported eyes.

197 L. M.

"Wash me thoroughly from my iniquity, and cleanse me from my sin." Ps. li. 2.

O THOU that hear'st when sinners cry,
Though all my crimes before thee lie,
Behold them not with angry look,
But blot their memory from thy book.

2 Though I have grieved thy Spirit, Lord,
Thy help and comfort still afford;
And let a wretch come near thy throne,
To plead the merits of thy Son.

3 A broken heart, my God, my King,
Is all the sacrifice I bring;
The God of grace will ne'er despise
A broken heart for sacrifice.

198 L. M.

"Therefore, being justified by faith, we have peace with God through our Lord Jesus Christ."
ROMANS v. 1.

PEACE, troubled soul, whose plaintive moan
Hath taught each scene the note of woe;
Cease thy complaint, suppress thy groan,
And let thy tears forget to flow;
Behold, the precious balm is found,
To lull thy pain, and heal thy wound.

2 Come, freely come, by sin opprest,
On Jesus cast thy weighty load;

In him thy refuge find, thy rest,
Safe in the mercy of thy God:
Thy God's thy Saviour, glorious word:
O hear, believe, and bless the Lord.

199 C. M.

"Now faith is the substance of things hoped for, the evidence of things not seen." HEB. xi. 1.

O FOR a faith that will not shrink,
Though pressed by many a foe;
That will not tremble on the brink
Of poverty or woe;

2 That will not murmur nor complain
Beneath the chastening rod;
But in the hour of grief or pain
Can lean upon its God.

3 A faith that keeps the narrow way,
By truth restrained and led,
And with a pure and heavenly ray
Lights up a dying bed.

4 Lord, give me such a faith as this,
And then, whate'er may come,
I'll taste e'en here the hallowed bliss
Of an eternal home.

200 7 s.

"As thy days, so shall thy strength be."
DEUT. xxxiii. 25.

WAIT, my soul, upon the Lord,
To his gracious promise flee,
Laying hold upon this word,
"As thy days, thy strength shall be."

2 If the sorrows of thy case
Seem peculiar still to thee,
God has promised needful grace,—
"As thy days, thy strength shall be."

3 Days of trial, days of grief,
In succession thou may'st see;
This is still my sweet relief,—
"As thy days, thy strength shall be."

4 Rock of ages, I'm secure,
With thy promise, full and free,
Faithful, positive, and sure;
"As thy days, thy strength shall be."

201 L. M.

"I will heal their backsliding, I will love them freely."
HOSEA xiv. 4.

WEARY of wandering from my God,
And now made willing to return,
I hear, and bow beneath the rod;
To him, with penitence I mourn:
I have an advocate above,
A friend before the throne of love.

2 O Jesus! full of truth and grace,
More full of grace than I of sin,
Yet once again I seek thy face,
Open thine arms and take me in;
O, freely my backslidings heal,
And love the dying sinner still.

202 L. M.

"Search me, O God, and know my heart: try me and know my thoughts; and see if there be any wicked way in me, and lead me in the way everlasting." Ps. cxxxix. 23, 24.

O THOU, to whose all-searching sight,
The darkness shineth as the light,
Search, prove my heart; it looks to thee,
O burst its bonds, and set it free.

2 Wash out its stains, remove its dross,
Bind my affections to the cross;
Hallow each thought, let all within
Be clean, as thou, my Lord, art clean.

3 If in this darksome wild I stray,
Be thou my light, be thou my way;
No foes, no violence I fear,
No harm, while thou, my God, art near.

4 When rising floods my soul o'erflow,
When sinks my heart in waves of woe,
Jesus, thy timely aid impart,
And raise my head, and cheer my heart.

5 Saviour, where'er thy steps I see,
Dauntless, untired, I follow thee:
O let thy hand support me still,
And lead me to thy holy hill.

203 C. M.

"Looking unto Jesus, the author and finisher of our faith." Heb. xii. 2.

LO! what a cloud of witnesses
Encompass us around,

Men once like us with suffering tried,
But now with glory crowned.

2 Let us, with zeal like theirs inspired,
Strive in the Christian race;
And, freed from every weight of sin,
Their holy footsteps trace.

3 Behold a witness nobler still,
Who trod affliction's path,
Jesus, the Author, Finisher,
Rewarder of our faith;

4 He, for the joy before him set,
And moved by pitying love,
Endured the cross, despised the shame,
And now he reigns above.

5 Thither, forgetting things behind,
Press we to God's right hand;
There, with the Saviour and his saints,
Triumphantly to stand.

204 S. M.

"Say ye to the righteous that it shall be well with him." ISAIAH iii. 10.

WHAT cheering words are these!
Their sweetness who can tell?
In time and to eternity,
'Tis with the righteous well.

2 In every state secure,
Kept by Jehovah's eye;

'Tis well with them while life endures,
And well when called to die.

3 'Tis well when joys arise;
'Tis well when sorrows flow;
'Tis well when darkness veils the skies,
And strong temptations blow.

4 'Tis well when at his throne
They wrestle, weep, and pray,
'Tis well when at his feet they groan,
Though grieved at his delay.

5 'Tis well when Jesus calls,
"From earth and sin arise,
Join with the hosts of ransomed souls,
Made to salvation wise."

205 C. M.

"My soul, wait thou only upon God; for my expectation is from him." Ps. lxii. 5.

WHILE thee I seek, protecting Power,
Be my vain wishes stilled;
And may this consecrated hour
With better hopes be filled.

2 Thy love the power of thought bestowed,
To thee my thoughts would soar;
Thy mercy o'er my life has flowed,
That mercy I adore.

3 In each event of life, how clear
Thy ruling hand I see;

Each blessing to my soul more dear,
Because conferred by thee.

4 In every joy that crowns my days,
In every pain I bear,
My heart shall find delight in praise,
Or seek relief in prayer.

5 When gladness wings my favoured hour,
Thy love my thoughts shall fill;
Resigned, when storms of sorrow lower,
My soul shall meet thy will.

6 My lifted eye, without a tear,
The gathering storm shall see;
My steadfast heart shall know no fear:
That heart will rest on thee.

206 S. M.

"Take unto you the whole armour of God, that ye may be able to withstand in the evil day, and having done all, to stand." EPH. vi. 13.

SOLDIERS of Christ, arise,
And put your armour on,
Strong in the strength which God supplies,
Through his eternal Son;

2 Strong in the Lord of Hosts,
And in his mighty power,
Who in the strength of Jesus trusts
Is more than conqueror.

3 Stand then in his great might,
With all his strength endued;
And take, to arm you for the fight,
The panoply of God;

4 That having all things done,
And all your conflicts past,
Ye may o'ercome through Christ alone,
And stand complete at last.

207 C. M.

"God is faithful, who will not suffer you to be tempted above that ye are able." 1 Cor. x. 13.

ALAS, what hourly dangers rise,
What snares beset my way;
To heaven, O let me lift mine eyes,
And hourly watch and pray.

2 Whene'er temptations fright my heart,
Or lure my feet aside,
My God, thy powerful aid impart,
My Guardian and my Guide.

3 O keep me in thy heavenly way,
And bid the tempter flee;
And let me never, never stray,
From happiness and thee.

208 C. M.

"Hast thou not known? hast thou not heard, that the everlasting God, the Lord, the Creator of the ends of the earth, fainteth not, neither is weary?" Isaiah xl. 28.

WHY mournest thou, my anxious soul,
Despairing of relief,
As if the Lord o'erlooked thy cares,
Or pitied not thy grief?

2 Hast thou not known, hast thou not heard,
That firm remains on high
The everlasting throne of him
Who made the earth and sky?

3 Art thou afraid his power will fail
In sorrow's evil day?
Can the Creator's mighty arm
Grow weary or decay?

4 Supreme in wisdom as in power
The Rock of Ages stands;
Thou canst not search his mind, nor trace
The working of his hands.

5 He gives the conquest to the weak,
Supports the fainting heart;
And courage in the evil hour
His heavenly aids impart.

6 Mere human energy shall faint,
And youthful vigour cease;
But those who wait upon the Lord
In strength shall still increase.

7 They with unwearied step shall tread
The path of life divine;
With growing ardour onward move,
With growing brightness shine.

8 On eagles' wings they mount, they soar
On wings of faith and love;
Till past the sphere of earth and sin
They rise to heaven above.

209 C. M.

"Her ways are ways of pleasantness, and all her paths are peace." PROV. iii. 17.

O, HAPPY is the man who hears
  Religion's warning voice,
And who celestial wisdom makes
  His early, only choice.

2 For she has treasures greater far
  Than east or west unfold;
More precious are her bright rewards
  Than gems, or stores of gold.

3 Her right hand offers to the just
  Immortal, happy days;
Her left, imperishable wealth,
  And heavenly crowns displays.

4 And, as her holy labours rise,
  So her rewards increase;
Her ways are ways of pleasantness,
  And all her paths are peace.

210 S. M.

"Ye were as sheep going astray; but are now returned unto the Shepherd and Bishop of your souls."
1 PETER ii. 25.

I WAS a wandering sheep,
  I did not love the fold;
I did not love my Father's voice,
  I would not be controlled;

I was a wayward child,
  I did not love my home,
I did not love my Shepherd's voice,
  I loved afar to roam.

2 The Shepherd sought his sheep,
  The Father sought his child;
They followed me o'er vale and hill,
  O'er deserts waste and wild;
They found me nigh to death,
  Famished, and faint, and lone;
They bound me with the bands of love,
  They saved the wandering one.

3 Jesus my Shepherd is,
  'Twas he that loved my soul,
'Twas he that washed me in his blood,
  'Twas he that made me whole;
'Twas he that sought the lost,
  That found the wandering sheep,
'Twas he that brought me to the fold,
  'Tis he that still doth keep.

4 No more a wandering sheep,
  I love to be controlled,
I love my tender Shepherd's voice,
  I love the peaceful fold;
No more a wayward child,
  I seek no more to roam,
I love my heavenly Father's voice,
  I love, I love his home.

211 11 s.

"I will sing aloud of thy mercy." Ps. lix. 16.

THY mercy, my God, is the theme of my song,
The joy of my heart, and the boast of my tongue;
Free grace hath alone, from the first to the last,
Secured my affections, and bound my soul fast.

2 Thy mercy has vanquished my obdurate heart,
That wonders to feel its own hardness depart:
Dissolved by thy goodness, I fall to the ground,
And weep to the praise of the mercy I've found.

3 The door of thy mercy stands open all day,
To the poor and the needy, who knock by the way;
No sinner shall ever a place be denied,
Who comes seeking mercy through Jesus that died.

4 Thy mercy in Jesus exempts me from hell;
Its glories I'll sing, and its wonders I'll tell:

'Twas Jesus, my friend, when he hung on
the tree,
Who opened the fountain of mercy for me.

212 C. M.

"Restore unto me the joy of thy salvation." Ps. li. 12.

O FOR a closer walk with God,
A calm and heavenly frame;
A light to shine upon the road
That leads me to the Lamb.

2 Where is the blessedness I knew,
When first I saw the Lord?
Where is the soul refreshing view
Of Jesus and his word?

3 Return, O holy Dove, return,
Sweet messenger of rest;
I hate the sins that made thee mourn,
And drove thee from my breast.

4 The dearest idol I have known,
Whate'er that idol be,
Help me to tear it from thy throne,
And worship only thee.

5 So shall my walk be close with God,
Calm and serene my frame;
So purer light shall mark the road
That leads me to the Lamb.

213 L. M.

"Casting all your care upon him; for he careth for you." 1 PETER v. 7.

BE still, my heart, these anxious cares
To thee are burdens, thorns, and snares;
They cast dishonour on thy Lord,
And contradict his gracious word.

2 Brought safely by his hand thus far,
Why wilt thou now give place to fear?
How canst thou want, if he provide,
Or lose thy way with such a guide?

3 When first before his mercy-seat
Thou didst to him thy all commit,
He gave thee warrant from that hour,
To trust his wisdom, love, and power.

4 Did ever trouble yet befall,
And he refuse to hear thy call?
And has he not his promise past,
That thou shalt overcome at last?

5 Though rough and thorny be the road,
It leads thee home, apace, to God;
Then count thy present trials small,
For heaven will make amends for all.

214 C. M.

"How unsearchable are his judgments, and his ways past finding out." ROMANS xi. 33.

GOD moves in a mysterious way
His wonders to perform;

He plants his footsteps in the sea,
  And rides upon the storm.

2 Deep in unfathomable mines,
  With never failing skill,
He treasures up his bright designs,
  And works his gracious will.

3 Ye fearful saints, fresh courage take;
  The clouds ye so much dread
Are big with mercy, and shall break
  In blessings on your head.

4 Judge not the Lord by feeble sense,
  But trust him for his grace:
Behind a frowning Providence
  He hides a smiling face.

5 His purposes will ripen fast,
  Unfolding every hour:
The bud may have a bitter taste,
  But sweet will be the flower.

6 Blind unbelief is sure to err,
  And scan his work in vain:
God is his own interpreter,
  And he will make it plain.

215 C. M.

"In all thy ways acknowledge him, and he shal. direct thy paths." PROV. iii. 6.

O THOU who didst uphold my way,
  From earliest infancy,
Before my lisping tongue could say,
  "Dear Lord, remember me!"

2 Still through the paths of youth my Guide
And my Protector be,
And when my feet would turn aside,
Dear Lord, remember me!

3 If thou shouldst pain or sickness send,
From murmuring keep me free;
Or if thy hand should riches lend,
Dear Lord, remember me.

4 And when this earthly scene I leave,
And worldly prospects flee,
As then my latest sigh I heave,
Dear Lord, remember me.

216 8, 7.

"For the promise is unto you and to your children."
ACTS ii. 39.

SAVIOUR, who thy flock art feeding,
With the shepherd's kindest care,
All the feeble gently leading,
While the lambs thy bosom share;

2 Now these little ones receiving,
Fold them in thy gracious arm;
There, we know, thy word believing,
Only there, secure from harm.

3 Never, from thy pasture roving,
Let them be the Lion's prey:
Let thy tenderness, so loving,
Keep them all life's dangerous way.

4 Then, within thy fold eternal,
  Let them find a resting place;
Feed in pastures ever vernal,
  Drink the rivers of thy grace.

217 — 7 s.

"O how love I thy law!" Ps. cxix. 97.

HOLY Bible! book divine!
  Precious treasure, thou art mine!
Mine, to tell me whence I came;
Mine, to teach me what I am.

2 Mine, to chide me when I rove:
Mine, to show a Saviour's love;
Mine art thou to guide my feet,
Mine, to judge, condemn, acquit.

3 Mine, to comfort in distress,
If the Holy Spirit bless;
Mine, to show by living faith
Man can triumph over death.

4 Mine, to tell of joys to come,
And the rebel sinner's doom,
O thou precious book divine,
Precious treasure, thou art mine!

218 — C. M.

"Let us hold fast our profession." Heb. iv. 14.

WITNESS, ye men and angels; now
  Before the Lord we speak;

To him we make a solemn vow,
 A vow we dare not break.

2 That, long as life itself shall last,
 Ourselves to Christ we yield;
Nor from his cause will we depart,
 Or ever quit the field.

3 We trust not in our native strength,
 But on his grace rely,
That, with returning wants, the Lord
 Will all our need supply.

4 Lord, guide our doubtful feet aright,
 And keep us in thy ways;
And, while we turn our vows to prayers,
 Turn thou our prayers to praise.

219 S. M.

"I am thine; save me, for I have sought thy precepts."
Ps. cxix. 94.

LORD, in the strength of grace,
 With a glad heart and free,
Myself, my residue of days,
 I consecrate to thee.

2 Thy ransomed servant, I
 Restore to thee thine own;
And from this moment live or die
 To serve my God alone.

220 L. M.

"Thy vows are upon me, O God; I will render praises unto thee." Ps. lvi. 12.

O HAPPY day, that stays my choice
On thee, my Saviour and my God;
Well may this glowing heart rejoice,
And tell thy goodness all abroad.

2 O happy bond, that seals my vows,
To him who merits all my love;
Let cheerful anthems fill his house,
While to his sacred throne I move.

3 'Tis done, the great transaction's done;
Deign, gracious Lord, to make me thine;
Help me through grace to follow on,
Glad to confess thy voice divine.

4 Here rest, my oft divided heart,
Fixed on thy God, thy Saviour, rest;
Who with the world would grieve to part
When called on angels' food to feast?

5 High heaven, that heard the solemn vow,
That vow renewed shall daily hear,
Till in life's latest hour I bow,
And bless in death a bond so dear.

CHORUS.

Happy day, happy day,
When Jesus washed my sins away;
He taught me how to watch and pray,
And live rejoicing every day.

221 L. M.

"In whom we have boldness and access with confidence by the faith of him." EPH. iii. 12.

JESUS, my all, to heaven is gone:
He whom I fix my hopes upon:
His track I see, and I'll pursue
The narrow way, till him I view.

2 This is the way I long have sought,
And mourned because I found it not;
My grief a burden long has been,
Because I was not saved from sin.

3 The more I strove against its power,
I felt its weight and guilt the more;
Till late I heard my Saviour say,
"Come hither, soul, I am the way."

4 Lo! glad I come; and thou, blest Lamb,
Shalt take me to thee as I am:
Nothing but sin have I to give,
Nothing but love shall I receive.

5 Then will I tell to sinners round,
What a dear Saviour I have found;
I'll point to thy redeeming blood,
And say, "Behold the way to God."

222 C. M.

"But now in Christ Jesus ye who sometime were far off are made nigh by the blood of Christ." EPH. ii. 13.

AND are we now brought near to God,
Who once at distance stood?

And to effect this glorious change,
Did Jesus shed his blood?

2 O for a song of ardent praise,
To bear our souls above!
What should allay our lively hope,
Or damp our flaming love?

3 Then let us join the heavenly choirs,
To praise our heavenly King:
O may that love which spread this board,
Inspire us while we sing,

4 "Glory to God in highest strains,
And to the earth be peace;
Good will from heaven to men is come,
And let it never cease."

223 L. M.

"This do in remembrance of me." LUKE xxii. 19.

MY God, and is thy table spread,
And does thy cup with love o'erflow?
Thither be all thy children led,
And let them thy sweet mercies know.

2 Hail sacred feast, which Jesus makes,
Rich banquet of his flesh and blood:
Thrice happy he who here partakes
That sacred stream, that heavenly food.

3 Why are its bounties all in vain
Before unwilling hearts displayed?

Was not for you the victim slain?
Are you forbid the children's bread?

4 O let thy table honoured be,
And furnished well with joyful guests:
And may each soul salvation see,
That here its holy pledges tastes.

5 Drawn by thy quickening grace, O Lord,
In countless numbers let them come
And gather from their Father's board,
The bread that lives beyond the tomb.

6 Nor let thy spreading gospel rest,
Till through the world thy truth has run;
Till with this bread all men be blest,
Who see the light or feel the sun

224 S. M.

"Behold how good and how pleasant it is for brethren to dwell together in unity." Ps. cxxxiii. 1.

LET party names no more
The Christian world o'erspread;
Gentile and Jew, and bond and free,
Are one in Christ their Head.

2 Among the saints on earth
Let mutual love be found;
Heirs of the same inheritance,
With mutual blessings crowned.

3 Thus will the church below
Resemble that above,
Where streams of pleasure ever flow,
And every heart is love.

225 S. M.

"That they all may be one, as thou, Father, art in me, and I in thee, that they also may be one in us."
JOHN xvii. 21.

WITH Jesus in our midst
We gather round the board;
Though many, we are one in Christ,
One body in the Lord.

2 Our sins were laid on him
When bruised on Calvary;
For us he died and rose again,
A pledge of victory.

3 Faith eats the bread of life,
And drinks the living wine;
Thus we, in love together knit,
On Jesus' breast recline.

4 Soon shall the night be gone,
And we with Jesus reign;
The marriage supper of the Lamb
Shall banish every pain.

226

"When that which is perfect is come, then that which is in part shall be done away." 1 Cor. xiii. 10.

SAY, brothers, will you meet us
On Canaan's happy shore?
By the grace of God we'll meet you
Where parting is no more.

2 Jesus lives and reigns forever
On Canaan's happy shore!
Glory, glory, hallelujah,
Forever, evermore!

227

"The things which are seen are temporal; but the things which are not seen are eternal."
2 Cor. iv. 18.

WHEN shall we meet again,
Meet ne'er to sever?
When will peace wreath her chain
Round us forever?
Our hearts will ne'er repose,
Safe from each blast that blows,
In this dark vale of woes,
Never, no, never.

2 When shall love freely flow,
Pure as life's river?
When shall sweet friendship glow
Changeless forever?

Where joys celestial thrill,
Where bliss each heart shall fill,
And fears of parting chill,
Never, no, never.

3 Up to that world of light,
Take us, dear Saviour,
May we all there unite,
Happy forever.
Where kindred spirits dwell,
There may our music swell,
And time our joys dispel,
Never, no, never.

228 — 7 s.

"Behold, he that keepeth Israel shall neither slumber nor sleep." Ps. cxxi. 4.

FOR a season called to part,
Let us now ourselves commend
To the gracious eye and heart
Of our ever present Friend.

2 Jesus, hear our humble prayer:
Tender Shepherd of thy sheep,
Let thy mercy and thy care
All our souls in safety keep.

229 — S. M.

"Keep yourselves in the love of God, looking for the mercy of our Lord Jesus Christ unto eternal life." Jude 21.

O WHERE shall rest be found,
Rest for the weary soul;

'Twere vain the ocean's depths to sound,
 Or pierce to either pole.

2 The world can never give
 The bliss for which we sigh;
'Tis not the whole of life to live,
 Nor all of death to die.

3 Beyond this vale of tears
 There is a life above,
Unmeasured by the flight of years;
 And all that life is love.

4 There is a death, whose pang
 Outlasts the fleeting breath:
O, what eternal horrors hang
 Around the second death.

5 Lord God of truth and grace,
 Teach us that death to shun,
Lest we be driven from thy face,
 For evermore undone.

230 C. M.

"He will swallow up death in victory; and the Lord God will wipe away tears from off all faces."
ISAIAH XXV. 8.

HEAR what the voice from heaven declares
 To those in Christ who die;
Released from all their earthly cares,
 They'll reign with him on high.

2 Then why lament departed friends,
Or shake at death's alarms?
Death's but the servant Jesus sends
To call us to his arms.

3 If sin be pardoned, we're secure,
Death hath no sting beside;
The law gave sin its strength and power:
But Christ, our ransom, died.

4 The graves of all his saints he blessed,
When in the grave he lay;
And, rising thence, their hopes he raised
To everlasting day.

5 Then, joyfully, while life we have,
To Christ, our life, we'll sing,
"Where is thy victory, O grave?
And where, O death, thy sting?"

231 L. M.

"Though I walk through the valley of the shadow of death, I will fear no evil: for thou art with me: thy rod and thy staff, they comfort me." Ps. xxiii. 4.

WHY should we start, and fear to die?
What timorous worms we mortals are:
Death is the gate of endless joy,
And yet we dread to enter there.

2 Jesus can make a dying bed
Feel soft as downy pillows are,
While on his breast I lean my head,
And breathe my life out sweetly there.

232 C. M.

"Every idle word that men shall speak, they shall give account thereof in the day of judgment."
MATT. xii. 36.

AND must I be to judgment brought,
And answer in that day
For every vain and idle thought,
And every word I say?

2 Thou awful Judge of quick and dead,
The watchful power bestow;
So shall I to my ways take heed,
To all I speak or do.

3 If now thou standest at the door,
O let me feel thee near!
And make my peace with God, before
I at thy bar appear.

233 7 s.

"These are they which came out of great tribulation, and have washed their robes, and made them white in the blood of the Lamb." REV. vii. 14.

WHO are these in bright array?
This innumerable throng,
Round the altar night and day
Tuning their triumphant song?
Worthy is the Lamb once slain,
Blessing, honour, glory, power,
Wisdom, riches, to obtain;
New dominion every hour.

2 These through fiery trials trod;
These from great affliction came
Now before the throne of God,
Sealed with his eternal Name:
Clad in raiment pure and white,
Victor palms in every hand,
Through their great Redeemer's might,
More than conquerors they stand.

3 Hunger, thirst, disease, unknown,
On immortal fruits they feed;
Them the Lamb amidst the throne
Shall to living fountains lead;
Joy and gladness banish sighs:
Perfect love dispels their fears;
And forever from their eyes
God shall wipe away their tears.

234

"We, according to his promise, look for new heavens and a new earth, wherein dwelleth righteousness."
2 PETER iii. 13.

THERE is a happy land,
Far, far away,
Where saints in glory stand,
Bright, bright as day;
O, how they sweetly sing,
Worthy is our Saviour King;
Loud let his praises ring,—
Praise, praise for aye.

2 Come to this happy land,
Come, come away;

Why will ye doubting stand—
  Why still delay?
O, we shall happy be,
When from sin and sorrow free,
Lord, we shall live with thee!
  Blest, blest for aye.

3 Bright in that happy land
  Beams every eye,—
Kept by a Father's hand,
  Love cannot die.
On, then, to glory! on!
Be a crown and kingdom won;
And bright above the sun,
  We reign for aye.

235 C. M.

"At thy right hand there are pleasures for evermore."
Ps. xvi. 11.

THERE is a land of pure delight,
  Where saints immortal reign;
Eternal day excludes the night,
  And pleasures banish pain.

2 There everlasting spring abides,
  And never-fading flowers;
Death, like a narrow sea, divides
  This heavenly land from ours.

3 Bright fields, beyond the swelling flood,
  Stand dressed in living green;
So to the Jews fair Canaan stood,
  While Jordan rolled between.

4 But timorous mortals start, and shrink
To cross the narrow sea;
And linger, trembling, on the brink,
And fear to launch away.

5 O, could we make our doubts remove
Those gloomy doubts that rise,
And see the Canaan that we love,
With faith's illumined eyes;

6 Could we but climb where Moses stood,
And view the landscape o'er;
Not Jordan's stream, nor death's cold flood
Should fright us from the shore.

236 C. M.

"To him that overcometh will I give to eat of the tree of life." Rev. ii. 7.

ON Jordan's stormy banks I stand,
And cast a wishful eye
To Canaan's fair and happy land,
Where my possessions lie.

2 O, the transporting, rapturous scene,
That rises to my sight!
Sweet fields arrayed in living green,
And rivers of delight.

3 O'er all those wide extended plains
Shines one eternal day;
There God the Son forever reigns,
And scatters night away.

4 When shall I reach that happy place,
And be forever blest?
When shall I see my Father's face,
And in his bosom rest?

237 S. M.

"A sabbath of rest to the Lord."
EXODUS xxxv. 2.

WELCOME, sweet day of rest,
That saw the Lord arise;
Welcome to this reviving breast,
And these rejoicing eyes!

2 The King himself comes near,
And feasts his saints to-day;
Here we may sit, and see him here,
And love, and praise, and pray.

3 One day amidst the place
Where Jesus is within,
Is better than ten thousand days
Of pleasure and of sin.

4 My willing soul would stay
In such a frame as this,
Till it is called to soar away
To everlasting bliss.

238 L. M.

"A delight, the holy of the Lord, honourable."
ISAIAH lviii. 13.

MY opening eyes with rapture see
The dawn of thy returning day;

My thoughts, O God, ascend to thee,
While thus my early vows I pay.

2 I yield my heart to thee alone,
Nor would receive another guest;
Eternal King, erect thy throne,
And reign sole monarch in my breast.

3 O bid this trifling world retire,
And drive each carnal thought away;
Nor let me feel one vain desire,
One sinful thought, through all the day.

4 Then, to thy courts when I repair,
My soul shall rise on joyful wing,
The wonders of thy love declare,
And join the strains which angels sing.

239 H. M.

"The sabbath of the Lord." LEV. xxiii. 3.

AWAKE, ye saints, awake,
And hail this sacred day;
In loftiest songs of praise
Your joyful homage pay;
Welcome the day that God hath blest,
The type of heaven's eternal rest.

2 On this auspicious morn
The Lord of life arose;
He burst the bars of death,
And vanquished all our foes:
And now he pleads our cause above,
And reaps the fruits of all his love.

3 All hail, triumphant Lord!
  Heaven with hosannas rings,
And earth, in humbler strains,
  Thy praise responsive sings:
Worthy the Lamb that once was slain,
Through endless years to live and reign.

4 Great King, gird on thy sword,
  Ascend thy conquering car;
While justice, truth, and love,
  Maintain thy glorious war.
This day let sinners own thy sway,
And rebels cast their arms away.

240 7s.

"If ye then be risen with Christ, seek those things which are above, where Christ sitteth on the right hand of God." Col. iii. 1.

CHRIST the Lord is risen to-day,
  Sons of men and angels say:
Raise your joys and triumphs high,
Sing, ye heavens, and earth reply.

2 Love's redeeming work is done,
Fought the fight, the victory won:
Jesus' agony is o'er,
Darkness veils the earth no more.

3 Vain the stone, the watch, the seal,
Christ has burst the gates of hell;
Death in vain forbids him rise,
Christ hath opened Paradise.

4 Soar we now where Christ hath led,
Following our exalted Head;
Made like him, like him we rise;
Ours the cross, the grave, the skies.

241 7 s.

"Ye shall keep my sabbaths, and reverence my sanctuary." Lev. xxvi. 2.

SAFELY through another week
God has brought us on our way;
Let us now a blessing seek,
Waiting in his courts to-day;
Day of all the week the best,
Emblem of eternal rest.

2 While we seek supplies of grace,
Through the dear Redeemer's name;
Show thy reconciling face,
Take away our sin and shame;
From our worldly cares set free,
May we rest this day in thee.

3 May the gospel's joyful sound
Conquer sinners, comfort saints,
Make the fruits of grace abound,
Bring relief from all complaints:
Thus let all our Sabbaths prove,
Till we join the church above.

242 L. M.

"I will sing aloud of thy mercy in the morning."
Ps. lix. 16.

AWAKE, my soul, and with the sun
Thy daily course of duty run;
Shake off dull sloth, and early rise
To pay thy morning sacrifice.

2 Wake, and lift up thyself, my heart,
And with the angels bear thy part;
Who all night long unwearied sing,
"Glory to thee, eternal King."

3 Glory to thee, who safe hast kept,
And hast refreshed me while I slept;
Grant, Lord, when I from death shall wake,
I may of endless life partake.

4 Lord, I my vows to thee renew;
Scatter my sins as morning dew;
Guard my first spring of thought and will,
And with thyself my spirit fill.

5 Direct, control, suggest this day,
All I design, or do, or say,
That all my powers, with all their might,
In thy sole glory may unite.

243 C. M.

"In the morning will I direct my prayer unto thee."
Ps. v. 3.

TO thee let my first offerings rise,
Whose sun creates the day,

Swift as his gladdening influence flies,
And spotless as his ray.

2 This day thy favouring hand be nigh,
So oft vouchsafed before;
Still may it lead, protect, supply,
And I that hand adore.

3 If bliss thy Providence impart,
For which, resigned, I pray,
Give me to feel a cheerful heart,
And grateful homage pay.

4 Affliction should thy love intend,
As vice or folly's cure,
Patient, to gain that gracious end,
May I the means endure.

5 Be this and every future day
Still wiser than the past;
And when I all my life survey,
May grace sustain at last.

244 7 s.

"And they rose up betimes in the morning."
GEN. xxvi. 31.

AT the golden rise of day,
Humbly, God, to thee we pray:
Uncreated Source of light,
Guide our thoughts and words aright.
Holy Father, at thy call
Light upon the earth did fall:
Speak the word again, and make
Morning o'er our hearts to break.

2 From the eternal Source in heaven
Light to us on earth be given,
Light of grace, to guard from wrath,
Light of faith, to guide our path.
Holy Spirit, let thy ray
Guide our footsteps, day by day,
While through earth's dark path we move
To eternal day above.

245 C. M.

"My voice shalt thou hear in the morning, O Lord."
Ps. v. 3.

ONCE more, my soul, the rising day
Salutes thy waking eyes:
Once more, my voice, thy tribute pay
To him who rules the skies.

2 'Tis he supports my mortal frame:
My tongue shall speak his praise;
My sins would rouse his wrath to flame,
And yet his wrath delays.

3 Great God, let all my hours be thine,
While I enjoy the light;
Then shall my sun in smiles decline,
And bring a peaceful night.

246 7 s.

"Be thou in the fear of the Lord all the day long."
Prov. xxiii. 17.

NOW the shades of night are gone;
Now the morning light is come;

Lord, may we be thine to-day;
Drive the shades of sin away.

2 Fill our souls with heavenly light,
Banish doubt and clear our sight;
In thy service, Lord, to-day,
May we labour, watch, and pray.

3 Keep our haughty passions bound,
Save us from our foes around;
Going out and coming in,
Keep us safe from every sin.

4 When our work of life is past,
O receive us then at last;
Night and sin will be no more,
When we reach the heavenly shore.

247 C. M.

"At noon will I pray, and cry aloud, and he shall hear my voice." Ps. lv. 18.

FROM busy toil and heavy care
We turn the weary mind;
And in the place of noontide prayer
Our sanctuary find.

2 The voice that stilled the stormy waves
On distant Galilee,
Speaks once again, and at the sound,
Retires another sea.

3 The restless waves of care and strife
Obey the mighty voice;
Peace broods the quiet waters o'er,
And all our souls rejoice.

4 These heaven-bright hours too soon are past;
Grant, Lord, this greater boon;
A place where worship never ends,
Nor night succeeds to noon.

CHORUS.

The mid-day hour, the noontide hour,
It is the hour of prayer;
Our souls receive renewing power,
For Jesus meets us there.

248 C. M.

"God is greatly to be feared in the assembly of the saints." Ps. lxxxix. 7.

JESUS, this mid-day hour of prayer
We consecrate to thee,
Forgetful of each earthly care,
We would thy glory see.

2 We come thy presence to implore:
O teach us how to pray!
Impart to us thy Spirit's power,
Thy saving grace display.

3 Baptize with energy divine
The contrite soul afresh;

O bow the stubborn will to thine,
  And give the heart of flesh.

4 Unite our hearts, unite our tongues,
  In lofty praise to thee,
Accept the tribute of our songs,
  Thou Holy One in Three.

249 L. M.

"In the night his song shall be with me, and my prayer unto the God of my life." Ps. xlii. 8.

GREAT God, to thee my evening song
  With humble gratitude I raise;
O let thy mercy tune my tongue,
  And fill my heart with lively praise.

2 My days unclouded as they pass,
  And every onward rolling hour,
Are monuments of wondrous grace,
  And witness to thy love and power.

3 And yet this thoughtless, wretched heart,
  Too oft regardless of thy love,
Ungrateful, can from thee depart,
  And from the path of duty rove.

4 Seal my forgiveness in the blood
  Of Christ, my Lord; his Name alone
I plead for pardon, gracious God,
  And kind acceptance at thy throne.

5 With hope in him mine eyelids close,
  With sleep refresh my feeble frame;
Safe in thy care may I repose,
  And wake with praises to thy Name.

250 C. P. M.

"Examine yourselves, whether ye be in the faith; prove your own selves." 2 COR. xiii. 5.

AT evening to my soul I say,
Come, give account for all the day,
Its moments, and its hours!
What rightly thought, or said, or done,
What grace attained, or knowledge won,
For whom employed thy powers?

2 What dying sinner hast thou warned,
And meekly prayed, though he hath scorned,
That Christ would him forgive?
In all, hast thou with single eye
Sought Christ alone to glorify,
For him alone to live?

251 7s.

"Let my prayer be set forth before thee as incense; and the lifting up of my hands, as the evening sacrifice." Ps. cxli. 2.

SOFTLY now the light of day
Fades upon my sight away;
Free from care, from labour free,
Lord, I would commune with thee:

2 Thou, whose all-pervading eye
Naught escapes, without, within,
Pardon each infirmity,
Open fault, and secret sin.

3 Soon for me the light of day
Shall forever pass away;
Then, from sin and sorrow free,
Take me, Lord, to dwell with thee:

4 Thou who, sinless, yet hast known
All of man's infirmity;
Then, from thine eternal throne,
Jesus, look with pitying eye.

252 L. M.

"Whoso putteth his trust in the Lord shall be safe."
PROV. xxix. 25.

GLORY to thee, my God, this night,
For all the blessings of the light:
Keep me, O keep me, King of kings,
Under thine own Almighty wings.

2 Forgive me, Lord, for thy dear Son,
The ills that I this day have done:
That with the world, myself, and thee,
I, ere I sleep, at peace may be.

3 Teach me to live that I may dread
The grave as little as my bed;
Teach me to die, that so I may
Triumphing rise at the last day.

4 O may my soul on thee repose,
And with sweet sleep mine eyelids close:
Sleep, that may me more vigorous make
To serve my God when I awake.

5 O when shall I, in endless day,
Forever chase dark sleep away,
And hymns divine with angels sing,
Glory to thee, eternal King?

253 L. M.

"Awake! awake! put on thy strength, O Zion."
ISAIAH lii. 1.

TRIUMPHANT Sion, lift thy head
From dust, and darkness, and the dead:
Though humbled long, awake at length,
And gird thee with thy Saviour's strength.

2 Put all thy beauteous garments on,
And let thy excellence be known;
Decked in the robes of righteousness,
The world thy glories shall confess.

3 No more shall foes unclean invade,
And fill thy hallowed walls with dread;
No more shall hell's insulting host
Their victory and thy sorrows boast.

4 God from on high has heard thy prayer,
His hand thy ruin shall repair:
Nor will thy watchful Monarch cease
To guard thee in eternal peace.

254 L. M.

"I will bring you out from the people, and will gather you out of the countries, wherein ye are scattered, with a mighty hand." EZEK. xx. 34.

DISOWNED of heaven, by man oppressed,
Outcast from Sion's hallowed ground,
Wherefore should Israel's sons, once blessed,
Still roam the scorning world around?

2 Lord, visit thy forsaken race,
Back to thy fold the wanderers bring,
Teach them to seek thy slighted grace,
And hail in Christ their promised King.

3 The veil of darkness rend in twain,
Which hides their Shiloh's glorious light;
The severed olive branch again
Firm to its parent stock unite.

4 Hail, glorious day, expected long!
When Jew and Greek one prayer shall pour;
With eager feet one temple throng,
With grateful praise one God adore.

255

7, 6.

"The earth shall be full of the knowledge of the Lord."
ISAIAH xi. 9.

THE morning light is breaking,
  The darkness disappears;
The sons of earth are waking
  To penitential tears:
Each breeze that sweeps the ocean
  Brings tidings from afar,
Of nations in commotion,
  Prepared for Zion's war.

2 See heathen nations bending
  Before the God we love,
And thousand hearts ascending
  In gratitude above;
While sinners, now confessing,
  The gospel call obey,
And seek the Saviour's blessing,—
  A nation in a day.

3 Blessed river of salvation,
  Pursue thy onward way;
Flow thou to every nation,
  Nor in thy richness stay;
Stay not till all the lowly
  Triumphant reach their home;
Stay not till all the holy
  Proclaim—the Lord is come.

256 7, 6.

"He shall have dominion from sea to sea, and from the river unto the ends of the earth." Ps. lxxii. 8.

HAIL to the Lord's anointed,
Great David's greater Son,
Hail in the time appointed,
His reign on earth begun!
He comes to break oppression,
To set the captive free;
To take away transgression,
And rule in equity.

2 He comes with succour speedy
To those who suffer wrong;
To help the poor and needy,
And bid the weak be strong;
To give them songs for sighing,
Their darkness turn to light,
Whose souls, condemned and dying,
Were precious in his sight.

3 For him shall prayer unceasing
And daily vows ascend;
His kingdom still increasing,
A kingdom without end:
The tide of time shall never
His covenant remove;
His name shall stand forever,
That name to us is LOVE.

257

7 s.

"He calleth to me out of Seir, Watchman, what of the night? Watchman, what of the night? And the watchman said, The morning cometh, and also the night." ISAIAH xxi. 11, 12.

WATCHMAN, tell us of the night,
What its signs of promise are.
"Traveller, o'er yon mountain's height,
See that glory beaming star!"
Watchman, does its beauteous ray
Aught of hope or joy foretell?
"Traveller, yes: it brings the day,
Promised day of Israel."

2 Watchman, tell us of the night;
Higher yet that star ascends.
"Traveller, blessedness and light,
Peace and truth its course portends."
Watchman, will its beams alone
Gild the spot that gave them birth?
"Traveller, ages are its own;
See! it bursts o'er all the earth."

3 Watchman, tell us of the night,
For the morning seems to dawn.
"Traveller, darkness takes its flight,
Doubt and terror are withdrawn."
Watchman, let thy wanderings cease;
Hie thee to thy quiet home.
"Traveller, lo! the Prince of Peace,
Lo! the Son of God is come."

258 7, 6.

"The mountains and the hills shall break forth before you into singing, and all the trees of the field shall clap their hands." ISAIAH lv. 12.

WHEN shall the voice of singing
Flow joyfully along?
When hill and valley, ringing
With one triumphant song,
Proclaim the contest ended,
And Him who once was slain
Again to earth descended
In righteousness to reign!

2 Then from the craggy mountains
The sacred shout shall fly;
And shady vales and fountains
Shall echo the reply;
High tower and lowly dwelling
Shall send the chorus round,
All hallelujah swelling,
In one eternal sound!

259 C. P. M.

"Freely ye have received, freely give."
MATT. x. 8.

WHEN, Lord, to this our western land,
Led by thy providential hand,
Our wandering fathers came,
Their ancient homes, their friends in youth,
Sent forth the heralds of thy truth,
To keep them in thy Name.

2 Then, through our solitary coast,
The desert features soon were lost;
Thy temples there arose;
Our shores, as culture made them fair,
Were hallowed by thy rites, by prayer,
And blossomed as the rose.

3 And O, may we repay this debt
To regions solitary yet,
Within our spreading land:
There, brethren, from our common home,
Still westward, like our fathers, roam;
Still guided by thy hand.

4 Saviour, we own this debt of love:
O shed thy Spirit from above,
To move each Christian breast;
Till heralds shall thy truth proclaim,
And temples rise to fix thy Name,
Through all our desert West.

260 — 7, 6.

"Go ye into all the world, and preach the gospel unto every creature." MARK xvi. 15.

FROM Greenland's icy mountains,
From India's coral strand,
Where Afric's sunny fountains
Roll down their golden sand;
From many an ancient river,
From many a palmy plain,
They call us to deliver
Their land from error's chain.

2 What though the spicy breezes
Blow soft o'er Ceylon's isle,
Though every prospect pleases,
And only man is vile?
In vain with lavish kindness
The gifts of God are strewn;
The heathen, in his blindness,
Bows down to wood and stone.

3 Shall we whose souls are lighted
With wisdom from on high,
Shall we, to men benighted,
The lamp of life deny?
Salvation! O Salvation!
The joyful sound proclaim,
Till earth's remotest nation
Has learned Messiah's name.

4 Waft, waft, ye winds, his story,
And you, ye waters, roll,
Till, like a sea of glory,
It spreads from pole to pole;
Till, o'er our ransomed nature,
The Lamb for sinners slain,
Redeemer, King, Creator,
In bliss returns to reign.

261 7, 6.

"This gospel of the kingdom shall be preached in all the world." MATT. xxiv. 14.

NOW be the gospel banner
In every land unfurled;

And be the shout Hosanna,
  Re-echoed through the world:
Till every isle and nation,
  Till every tribe and tongue,
Receive the great salvation,
  And join the happy throng.

2 What though the embattled legions
  Of earth and hell combine?
His arm throughout their regions
  Shall soon resplendent shine:
Ride on, O Lord, victorious!
  Immanuel, Prince of Peace!
Thy triumph shall be glorious,
  Thine empire still increase.

3 Yes, thou shalt reign forever,
  O Jesus, King of kings!
Thy light, thy love, thy favour,
  Each ransomed captive sings:
The isles for thee are waiting,
  The deserts learn thy praise,
The hills and valleys greeting,
  The song responsive raise.

262

"They shall speak of the glory of thy kingdom, and talk of thy power." Ps. cxlv. 11.

YE servants of God,
  Your master proclaim,
And publish abroad
  His wonderful name:

The name all victorious
  Of Jesus extol;
His kingdom is glorious,
  And rules over all.

2 God ruleth on high,
  Almighty to save;
And still he is nigh;
  His presence we have:
The great congregation
  His triumph shall sing,
Ascribing salvation
  To Jesus our King.

3 Then let us adore
  And give him his right;
All glory and power,
  And wisdom and might;
All honour and blessing
  With angels above,
And thanks never ceasing,
  And infinite love.

263 8, 7.

"Glory to God in the highest, and on earth peace, good will towards men." LUKE ii. 14.

HARK! what mean those holy voices,
  Sweetly sounding through the skies?
Lo! the angelic host rejoices—
  Heavenly hallelujahs rise.

2 Jesus, our Lord, arise,
Scatter our enemies;
Now make them fall!
Let thine almighty aid
Our sure defence be made,
Our souls on thee be stayed;
Lord, hear our call!

3 Come, thou incarnate Word,
Gird on thy mighty sword;
Our prayer attend!
Come, and thy people bless;
Come, give thy word success;
Spirit of holiness,
On us descend!

265 7 s.

"Praise ye the Lord." Ps. cl. 1.

SONGS of praise the angels sang;
Heaven with hallelujahs rang,
When Jehovah's work begun,
When he spake and it was done.

2 Songs of praise awoke the morn
When the Prince of Peace was born;
Songs of praise arose, when he
Captive led captivity.

3 Heaven and earth must pass away;
Songs of praise shall crown that day;
God will make new heavens and earth;
Songs of praise shall hail their birth.

4 And shall man alone be dumb,
Till that glorious kingdom come?
No: the church delights to raise
Psalms, and hymns, and songs of praise.

5 Saints below, with heart and voice,
Still in songs of praise rejoice;
Learning here, by faith and love,
Songs of praise to sing above.

6 Borne upon their latest breath,
Songs of praise shall conquer death;
Then, amidst eternal joy,
Songs of praise their powers employ.

266 7 s.

"Let the children of Zion be joyful in their King."
Ps. clxix. 2.

GREAT the joy when Christians meet;
Christian fellowship, how sweet,
When, their theme of praise the same,
They exalt Jehovah's name!

2 Sing we, then, eternal love;
Such as did the Father move:
He beheld the world undone;
Loved the world, and gave his Son.

3 Sing the Son's unbounded love;
How he left the realms above;
Took our nature and our place,
Lived and died to save our race.

4 Sing we, too, the Spirit's love;
With our stubborn hearts he strove;
Chased the mists of sin away,
Turned our night to glorious day.

5 Great the joy, the union sweet,
When the saints in glory meet;
Where the theme is still the same;
Where they praise Jehovah's name.

267 11 s.

"Who is over all, God blessed forever."
ROMANS ix. 5.

O FATHER Almighty, to thee be addressed,
With Christ and the Spirit, one God ever blessed,
All glory and worship from earth and from heaven,
As was, and is now, and shall ever be given.

SUBJECTS.

INDEX.

A

INDEX.

B

C

D

E

F

G

H

INDEX.

I

J

L

M

N

INDEX.

O

P

INDEX.

R

S

T

INDEX.

Y

www.ingramcontent.com/pod-product-compliance
Lightning Source LLC
LaVergne TN
LVHW011205110826
845150LV00006B/1328

* 9 7 8 1 4 2 5 5 1 8 7 9 0 *